GARY FERGUSON
Research coordinated by Jane Ferguson

A Journey Through

SIMON & SCHUSTER
New York   London   Toronto   Sydney   Tokyo   Singapore

WALKING DOWN

the Yellowstone Rockies

THE
WILD

SIMON & SCHUSTER
Simon & Schuster Building
Rockefeller Center
1230 Avenue of the Americas
New York, New York 10020

Copyright ©1993 by Gary Ferguson
All rights reserved
including the right of reproduction
in whole or in part in any form.
SIMON & SCHUSTER and colophon are
registered trademarks of Simon & Schuster Inc.
Designed by Edith Fowler
Manufactured in the United States of America

10 9 8 7 6 5 4 3 2 1

Library of Congress Cataloging-in-Publication Data

Ferguson, Gary, 1956-
    Walking down the wild : a journey through the
    Yellowstone Rockies / Gary Ferguson.
        p.   cm.
    1. Backpacking—Rocky Mountain Region.
2. Backpacking—Yellowstone National Park. 3.
Rocky Mountain Region—Description and travel. 4.
Yellowstone National Park.   I. Title.
GV199.42.R62F46   1993
796.5'1'0978—dc20   92-42716   CIP
ISBN: 0-671-76851-4

ACKNOWLEDGMENTS

A special thanks goes to the staff of Montana State University, Eastern Montana College, and Yellowstone National Park. Also to the Greater Yellowstone Coalition, the Northern Plains Resource Council, and to many working on the ground in the national forests of the Yellowstone ecosystem. Finally, thanks to Wynn Miller for a steady editing hand, Bob Winslow for his encouragement, and to all my trail partners—Jane, Jim, Nancy, Martha, Eric, Verlynn, and John.

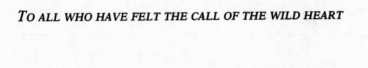

To all who have felt the call of the wild heart

The man killed the bird,
and with the bird he killed the song,
and with the song, himself.

FROM A PYGMY LEGEND

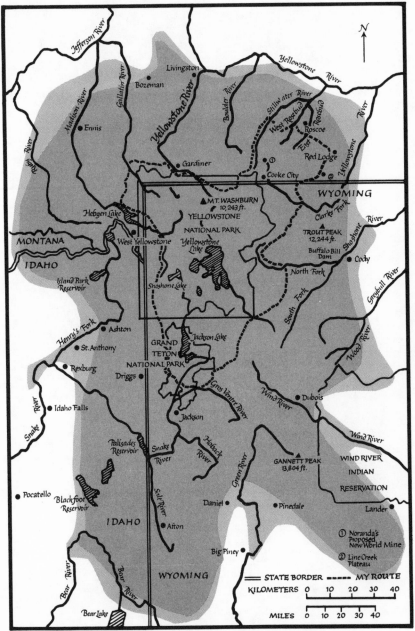

Greater Yellowstone Ecosystem

Ecosystem Core   Transition Zone

INTRODUCTION

*... I for one will cheerfully confess that I have derived no little
benefit from the frequent arguments and debates held in what
we termed the Rocky Mountain College, and I doubt not but
some of my comrades who considered themselves Classical
scholars have had some little added to their wisdom in these
assemblies, however rude they might appear.*

> OSBORNE RUSSELL, trapper wintering near the fork
> of the Yellowstone and
> Clarks Fork rivers, 1837

Higher education at its best. The students a dozen grizzled
men huddling from the slap of a Montana winter in buffalo-
skin lodges, the northern lights pouring blood red across the
sky above them, and the trees, as Russell himself once described them, "cracking like pistols" in the bitter cold.
Though few could even write, there they squatted by the fire
night after night, reviving all the great notions that had come
to them the previous autumn on a thousand miles of wild
mountain trail. If nothing else, theirs was a school with passion—a place where the days shone with the strange luster
that builds when fear and wonder meet, a place where even
devout heathens might suddenly unravel fiery, earthbound
religions as bright and full of promise as the Rockies themselves. "They were adrift," writes historian David Lavender,
"and they liked it."

Much of what little remains of Russell's Rocky Mountain College will be found in the Yellowstone Rockies. It survives in the sweat and breath of men and women who grunt for two days with fifty-pound packs just to reach a blank spot on the map, or in those who huddle with bottles of schnapps in snow caves on March nights and yip with the coyotes, cocking their ears on occasion to the sound of avalanches highballing like freight trains down the side of some nearby canyon. It survives in lost skiers picking their way through lodgepole forests under the cold blaze of Orion, or with hikers in grizzly country, who bolt awake at three A.M. to the sound of branches snapping outside their tents.

Yet those most tightly bound to these wild, hallowed halls of education are troubled—troubled about mad dashes being made to drill oil wells on the greatest sweep of alpine tundra in the continental United States; troubled about the Church Universal and Triumphant digging bomb shelters in the floor of the Paradise Valley to hide from the communists; troubled about mines poised at the headwaters of major river systems, churning the earth for gold. The same region that scientists have long proclaimed the "largest essentially intact temperate ecosystem in the world" has literally dozens of separate identified threats to its integrity—a fact that in 1988 led the Wilderness Society to place Yellowstone Park on its list of the ten most endangered national parks in America. Ninety percent of all nonwilderness and wilderness study lands on the adjacent Bridger-Teton National Forest—nearly 2 million acres—is now open for oil and gas leasing. Over the next twenty years just two mining companies in the northeast portion of the ecosystem will unearth more than 40 million tons of ore—enough rock to fill the Rose Bowl five times over.

That much of the region is still untrammeled, there can be no doubt. As any backcountry junkie will tell you, there are plenty of places left where, but for the occasional jet trail leaking into the big sky, the land seems to have been somehow cast adrift from the moorings of the modern world. The seasons push and pull through the high country with the rhythm of thousands of years behind them. Herds of big game ebb and flow across the land. Winters rage. Fires burn. Indeed, it's the high level of wildness here that so far has allowed anxieties over development to remain more a cry for action than a call for eulogies. But the level of change rolling across this land has reached a pace never seen before. The raw essence of the Yellowstone Rockies, that something that novelist Willa Cather said could be breathed "only on the bright edges of the world," is slowly but surely drifting out of reach.

All of this is a far cry from the state of affairs that I hung my heart on as a kid growing up in the Midwest. I remember night after night huddling in the basement of my parents' house, poring over gas station maps of Montana and Wyoming, the winter storms outside raging off the waters of Lake Michigan like wild horses. Before I was twelve I'd memorized the location of every single road that lay twisted on the paper like strings of cooked spaghetti. These were the mountain passes, and I could imagine each one crawling up through pine and rock and sky. When summer came, and the air was sticky and full of the smell of cut grass, I'd walk four blocks to the River Park Library. There, in a quiet, poorly lit corner, waited Federal Writer's Project Guides highlighting the Yellowstone of the 1930s, as well as a rather queer assortment of oversized photo books with titles like *Vacationland U.S.A.* and *Beautiful America*—all with pictures of scrubbed families dressed in plaid shirts smiling down some Rocky Mountain roadside overlook. Sitting there on that old wooden floor, the place spiked with the heady smell of dust and paper, I found that I could drop clean off the face of Indiana. Suddenly I was a thousand miles west of Uniroyal and Bendix and Dodge and the endless parade of cornfields that had no appeal whatsoever except in late July and August, when the stalks were finally tall enough that a person wandering around carelessly just might become lost in them.

I could hardly have realized it at the time, but ultimately it was these images that I gathered as a child, that strange stewpot of fantasy and Kodachrome, that would direct much of my adult life. It was these images that drove me to study environmental science, that led me into my first job as a naturalist, that sent me running wide-eyed and open-mouthed up and down the Rocky Mountains for the last ten years, finally ending up on the doorstep of Yellowstone—one of the last truly wild places in America.

Given that history, it came as no surprise that one day I would decide to embark on a five-hundred-mile journey by foot through the Yellowstone Rockies. For one thing, I knew that such a trek would offer me an opportunity to gather what old-timers sometimes call "native wisdom." (For those unfamiliar with the term, native wisdom is knowledge of a place gained through personal experience—actually seeing, touching, hearing, and smelling the rhythms that roll across its nooks and crannies. Of course, the place doesn't need to be as big as the Yellowstone Rockies. Psychiatrist M. Scott Peck points out that even a man in love with his garden may at some point feel the garden becoming a part of him—"part of his identity, part of his history, part of his wisdom.") I want to know that when Mount Maurice has a cap of clouds on, it will probably be raining in an hour. When I catch sight of a hundred elk heading toward winter range, I'd like to be able to say whether they're early or late. I'd like to feel the satisfaction that comes from seeing that, after a year's absence, Barney the bald eagle is back wintering in his favorite cottonwood along the Clarks Fork River.

In the end, though, it wasn't just a quest for native wisdom that sent me to the canyons and caldera of the Yellowstone, through its thick green forests and stark black firescapes. There was another, perhaps bigger part of me that took to the trail to confront the feeling of desperation I've had as of late over how rapidly this place is disappearing. Of course, all things change. But to bid farewell to the last of anything, be it the final passenger pigeon or a great web of native landscape, is to feel a hard plug of sadness rising up from somewhere between the head and heart, a place that seems all but lost to modern man. For years I've squelched the anguish of the West by sticking close to the pristine, by committing to memory the spirit of the last, trackless vistas and then running them through my mind like a rose-colored mantra. But there comes a time when such framing begins to turn the earth into nothing more than a greeting card, when it leaves you no more connected to a place than you are to the glossy images on the nature calendar that hangs on your kitchen wall.

For 150 years the American West has been a kind of adolescent fantasy—a forever landscape, a place to fly footloose dreams like kites in the wind. But times have aged us. And when one is grown, as historian Roy Helton points out, one can no longer indulge with impunity in the follies of youth. Walking with both eyes open through this landscape is like sitting by the bedside of a dying friend, hoping in some childish way that something said, some small thing done, might help bring a little measure of relief. There's a part of me that still thinks such optimism isn't entirely unfounded. But I also realize that to hope is to seek comfort, to establish some kind of connection from which one day I might better understand the need for the passing away of precious things.

Curiously, right now there's an interesting parallel to what's happening in the Yellowstone Rockies going on half a world away. Six thousand years of nomadic life in the outback of Israel are coming to a close, as the government prompts the Arab bedouins to trade their drifting life-style for permanent homes in cinder block towns. "The hills I looked out on as a child had the rounded shapes of tents and camels," explains the principal of a bedouin secondary school. "Now the soft contours have given way to the stark cubes of the block houses. It reflects a new mind-set. Now we're thinking in cubes; we're thinking in frames that have already been made."

And so too is our thinking growing a little narrower day by day. The horizon of the American West is framed more and more not by wild, ragged patches of stone and timber, but by clear-cuts and mine tailings, by housing developments, by oil derricks blazing in what only yesterday was a dark and secret sky.

ONE

It's early morning on August 27. Highway 78 out of Red Lodge seems to float across the warm brown hills of south-central Montana like a good dream, spinning and turning through the grassy nips and tucks of the high plains. To the east the land drops gently across a series of broken swells and grass-covered coulees, each one still thick with the buzz of summer. It's hard to imagine that in just a couple of months this will be a dazzling snow-dune desert, a weave of white hills pitching and yawing across the prairie for three hundred miles before finally coming to rest on the cold, dry breast of the Dakotas.

Yet it's the view not to the east but to the west that holds me spellbound. For it's there that the mighty Beartooth Mountains rise, forming the northeastern limits of the Yellowstone Rockies. The Beartooths were among the first major peaks early nineteenth-century Americans and French Canadian trappers caught sight of as they made their long, dangerous treks westward along the Yellowstone searching for furs. A hundred years later, it was these mountains that made thousands of Midwesterners driving the Yellowstone Motor Trail steer their dusty, bug-covered Fords and Franklins to the side of the road and grab for their Kodaks. No matter how jaded a traveler you may be, there's no getting around the fact that these are staggering mountains—2 million acres of tundra and granite and ice towering fully seven thousand feet above the plains. Even the names given by early explorers and settlers speak to the bold, fierce character of the range: Forsaken Lake, Hellroaring Plateau, Froze-to-Death Mountain, Lonesome Lake, Lake of the Clouds, Lake of the Winds.

Jane and I drive north along the face of the Beartooths for twenty miles, merely flirting with them, before finally turning west at the town of Roscoe. Sitting there beside East Rosebud Creek under a flutter of cottonwood leaves is a woman in her sixties, dressed in blue jeans and a worn denim jacket. She smiles into the sunlit water, looking up only long enough for a quick wave as we pass, then returning her attention to the quiver of whitewater. A kingfisher suddenly swoops down from a tree branch, leveling out barely four feet above her head. She never notices.

There's a certain calmness, a kind of matter-of-fact freshness to the town of Roscoe, although, with a population of fifty, if you blink you can miss both the town and the feeling. Interestingly, Roscoe didn't used to be Roscoe at all. The first postmaster for the town was a man named Tim George, who, after years of tending to the mail from a bureau drawer in the parlor of his home, finally got a real post office in 1901. The honor of naming the postal station, and thus the town, went to George's sister Nancy, who was thought to be the first white woman to have settled in the area. In honor of her husband, Robert Morris, Nancy settled on the name Morris.

Unfortunately, confusion arose between the town of Morris and the town of Norris, named for another pioneer ranching family living a hundred miles to the west. People kept mucking things up by writing "Morris" on their envelopes in such a way that it read like "Norris," or writing "Norris" so that it looked like "Morris"—not to mention the fact that some of the mail meant for the Morrises in Morris instead ended up with the Norrises in Norris. (Thankfully, at the time Norris had no Morris nor did Morris have a Norris.) After a few years the postal service had had quite enough of this; since Morris was named ten years after Norris, one day Nancy was asked to select another name for her community. Of course she was disappointed, but being a practical woman she never balked. The first commandment of Western water law, after all—first in time, first in right—seemed just as fair when you applied it to the naming of towns. Thinking long and hard about the matter, Nancy suddenly recalled a horse she was especially fond of by the name of Roscoe. And the rest is history.

Besides the post office, there's only one obvious business in Roscoe—the Grizzly Bar. And a fine bar it is, with thick Angus steaks and cold bottled beer, and heaping relish plates that come to your table on trays the size of meat platters. As we drive past I have a strong urge to stop in for one of those icy beers, to raise a toast to the five hundred miles of trail that lie ahead. But it's not even eight in the morning, and no one is around but Stasha, an old black Labrador retriever that serves as official floor warmer and hospitality steward for the bar. I honk. Stasha blinks. We round the corner and are out of town.

Out of Roscoe at the end of a bone-shaking road is East Rosebud Lake—a cold, shimmering pool set like a sapphire between the granite toes of the east Beartooths. Immediately behind this lake lies one of the most splendid canyons in the West. Even from Highway 78, which lies a good dozen miles to the east, it's a magnificent sight, made more so on those summer afternoons when the caboose of a big thunderstorm comes rolling out from between the four-thousand-foot-high walls. It is a nineteenth-century Albert Bierstadt painting incarnate—an idyllic, ethereal image that seems more the work of mind than of matter.

But today we pass up the lure of the East Rosebud, instead turning north onto a little ranch road carefully etched across the grassy skin of the foothills. This route runs generally parallel to Highway 78, but is smaller and quieter. (Along this stretch of road we might see only one vehicle, whereas in ten miles of Highway 78 there could be as many as five or six!)

The longer I live in Montana, the more hopelessly lost in gravel I seem to get. Not long after moving west in 1977, I found myself leaving the cush of interstates for the frontage roads that commonly run alongside them. But pretty soon that wasn't enough, and I started selecting whatever other paved routes were open to me, whether they happened to make a straight line from point A to point B or not, which of course they never did. Before long even that wasn't far enough removed, so I opted for dirt and gravel—the roads that, if they show up on state maps at all, appear not as blue highways but as meandering braids of open lines, very often stamped with the enticing warning that one shouldn't venture onto them without first checking with locals for current conditions.

"How's the road to Elk City?"
"Depends on if it's raining on the divide."
"That happen a lot this time of year?"
"Hasn't rained there for going on two months now."
"So the road's probably in good shape."
"Well, it was until the rockslide last week."
"So I should forget it."
"I wouldn't say that. Jim Franks lives up there, and he's probably cleared it by now."
"So you think a van can make it?"
"Kinda depends on whether Jim was drunk or not when he cleared it."

Coming from a good, overly clean Lutheran household in the Midwest, carried through childhood across the asphalt in a freshly washed Chevrolet, I will admit that dirt roads used to bother me. For most of the summer and into the fall, thick puffs of dust waft up through the floor vents, not to mention the fact that the washboard surfaces shake loose the screws in the doors and dashboard until the whole car rattles like a can of stove bolts. Yet to me the landscape looks more appealing when whatever thoroughfares that cross it do so somewhat tentatively—when the straight, bladed lines are not of conquering proportions, but barely manage to maintain their hedge against the sprout of sage and the etch of rills and gullies.

We roll quietly past the Top Hat Ranch and Fiddler Creek,

past Fishtail Butte and the Buffalo Jump, and lastly along the beautiful Stillwater River to that final, somewhat startling slap of civilization, the Stillwater platinum-palladium mine. Though this joint Chevron-Manville operation has processed a thousand tons of ore a day for several years, the company is now pushing to double that for the remaining eighteen-year life of the project. The route past the mine was actually one of the first back roads we stumbled across after moving to Montana, and I remember thinking that this scene summed up the future of the northern Rockies as well as any could— a cold braid of steel fence, percolation ponds, and windowless tin buildings held against some of the wildest, most fabulous mountain scenery I'd ever laid eyes on. If the mountains meant spirit, the mine meant bread. And clothes. And mortgage and utility payments, alimony checks, a new school, and on some weeks, enough change left over for a few beers at the Chrome Bar.

For two years the paychecks arrived right on time. And then, in 1991, roughly a third of the work force was laid off. Absarokee fathers, once bright with optimism, started wringing their hands over the loss of demand for housing, over whether those who remained would be able to pay for that beautiful new high school. Most people tend to think of mining operations only in terms of environmental consequences, and there are certainly those here at Stillwater. Some biologists, for example, expect the resident herd of bighorn to vanish entirely within the next ten years, and bear-hunting season may be closed altogether. There are also concerns over water quality, as the mine recently petitioned the State Department of Health for the right to degrade the pristine nature of the Stillwater River. On another company project nearby, this one on the beautiful East Boulder River, requests have already been submitted to build a tailings dam with a slope gradient never before allowed in the state of Montana—a gradient that engineers say would increase the chance of collapse by "only" 12 percent. Yet by its very nature, big-business mining can also have serious consequences for workers. Should you buy that new truck, or will Chevron shut part of the operation down next month to put the company in a better tax position? Do you take out that home improvement loan, knowing that if sanctions are lifted on South Africa and the price of platinum falls, you probably won't be able to make the payments?

While much of the rest of the country has only recently started to feel the psychic consequences of these kinds of job-related roller-coaster rides, people in the intermountain West have been hanging on with white knuckles for a good hundred years. Boom and bust is a way of life here. What *has* changed in recent times, however, is the depth and degree to which extractive companies are using economic changes to blast, and ultimately weaken, environmental policy. Pointing the finger for job losses at "tree huggers" accomplishes a great deal. First, it solidifies a company's own workers by pitting them against a common enemy. Secondly, if the slam campaigns are run well—and most are—over time politicians and state agencies tend to become less likely to enforce environmental protection laws to the letter because they fear short-term corporate reprisals. If the companies play their cards right, lawmakers will sometimes even change legislation entirely, or if not, at least hand out exemptions like they were so many seed catalogs.

It's no accident that my journey through the Yellowstone Rockies will encompass many of the national forest lands surrounding the park. Although Yellowstone is the largest national park in the continental United States, it neither endures nor inspires on its own. Its boundaries were drawn at a time when few people understood the needs of bison and bears and elk, and even fewer understood how our own spirits could be broken as the less celebrated lands that cradle the park are exploited and fractured. Unless we can come to terms with the fact that these surrounding runs of river and pine and the high, rugged peaks and plateaus are merely appendages of a single system, then there's little chance of us saving either the biological or the psychological substance of what we know as Yellowstone.

Having spent a good six months talking to some seasoned

backcountry rats, I've emerged with a loosely woven plan for my trek. From the end of the Stillwater River Road I'll walk southwestward up the remaining length of the river to Abundance Basin, and then follow the north boundary of Yellowstone Park generally westward for fifty miles to the massive bulwarks of the Gallatin Range. In a subsequent trip I'll drop through Carrott Basin, a lonely, yawning stretch of meadowland where elk can be found running like ponies through fields of spring beauties and glacier lilies. From there my route will wind through the southwestern corner of Yellowstone Park and into the heart of Grand Teton. Making a U turn north of Jackson, Wyoming, I'll work my way back to the northeast through the Gros Ventre Range and along the rugged, windswept Absaroka Mountains—the land of the bighorn and the grizzly—across the alpine tundra of the Beartooth Plateau, and finally down Maurice Creek to the Rock Creek Valley.

Of course you could see a great deal of this country without ever leaving your bucket seat. But as in all wild places, here the best connections rise through the rhythm of feet falling on the earth. Thoreau, for whom ambling by foot was an art, liked to refer to his wildland walks as "sauntering." He explains that the word first appeared in the Middle Ages, when people roved about the country asking for charity under the pretense of going to the Holy Land. "There goes a Sainte-Terrer!" children would cry—a saunterer, a holy-lander.

It works for me. When I go sauntering in these mountains I often feel like some kind of pilgrim. True, I don't come looking for the birthplace of deities. But there are moments when it's possible to find what seems like some form of divine expression here—in a summer blizzard on the crest of the Absarokas, in the hot flick of lightning in the crown of a ponderosa, in the terror of a grizzly standing on her hind legs snapping her jaws at you. Walking these mountains is not necessarily a way to feel comfortable. But it's definitely a way to feel alive.

Standing in the parking lot, Jane and I inhale the dry, piney musk of Douglas fir and lodgepole for a moment, and then open the tailgate and drag out our backpacks. The two of us together shoulder about ninety-five pounds—not all that much by modern standards, but a far cry from old John O' the Mountains Muir, who did quite nicely with no more than a blanket, some bread, a few tea bags and a pot. As I close up my pack again, the somewhat disturbing thought dawns on me that when you come right down to it, the two of us have traded our time for money—money that we then use to buy expensive outdoor equipment to help ease our office-bound bones back into the wilds with as little pain as possible. True, Muir may have had to curl up closer to the fire at night to keep warm, may have on occasion had to huddle under an Engelmann spruce to stay dry in a rainstorm. But for a great part of his life he felt the full, ripe joy of the wilderness. As I slip the padded straps over my shoulders, I recall a comment Muir once made about being richer than the great financier E. H. Harriman: "I have all the money I want," he explained. "And he doesn't."

I peer through the dusty back window of the car one last time to make sure we didn't forget anything, snug up the pack with a good yank on the cinch straps, and totter off. We reach the trailhead just as a young man is coming out. He looks to be in his early twenties, with an old Gerry frame pack and shoulder-length hair hanging down to the collar of a faded yellow T-shirt that says "Go Climb a Rock." He's the spitting image of a good trip—a week's worth of whiskers, a few stray cuts on his legs from climbing rocks, and skin as brown as the dust on his leather boots. He wears an easy smile, but at the same time he looks a little melancholy. Wilderness lag, I figure—that sense of disorientation that spills through hikers when their wild time peters out in a parking lot lined with Chevrolets and Subarus.

"Nice day," I offer. "Have a good hike?"

"It was fantastic!" he begins with gusto, but then stops short, as if suddenly he realizes that there's really no way to explain exactly why it was so great. Finally he continues, detailing all the lakes and trails and peaks along his route, but none of it with the same sparkle that was in his voice a minute ago. Maybe after a long stint of solitude it's unsettling for him to be talking so much, trying to squeeze what must have been a grand adventure into an exchange of pleasantries with a couple of strangers. I decide to change the subject and begin to tell him of our planned route toward Cooke City. Suddenly he lights up again. "Last year I walked to Cooke," he says. "Amazing. Went right through the Storm Creek burn."

The Storm Creek fire was one of the biggest of that long, sizzling summer of 1988. Started by a hot flick of lightning, this was the blaze that almost obliterated Cooke City—the one that blew into town so fast that it nearly bit the tails off a string of pack horses and their cowboy outfitter, sending them all bolting down the highway in a camera shot that made producers of the six o'clock news swoon. On August 20, or "Black Sunday," as it's now called, eighty-mile-per-hour winds shoved the Storm Creek fire through ten miles of forest in less than three hours.

"So what does the country look like?" Jane asks.

"Well, the timber is pretty crisp. But in places the grass is thick enough to feed an elk convention. Funny thing. A friend of mine who works for the Forest Service said he came across that burn when it was so small he could've put it out by pissing on it."

"So why didn't he?" I ask, struck by the image of a courageous wilderness guard dashing up a hill with his fly open to relieve himself on a burning snag.

"Well, it was in the wilderness, and the management plan was to let natural fires burn there. Everyone says that's stupid. But hell, if Smoky Bear hadn't spent the last fifty years dousing every lightning strike he could get his paws on, there wouldn't have been the wood there to burn in the first place. The way I see it, it was a matter of time."

Around here opinions about the 1988 fires are easier to get than mosquito bites; we've managed to collect our first before even setting foot on the trail. Soon the hiker says good-bye and ambles over to an old gray Nova, the red bronc rider on his Wyoming license plate bleached by the sun into a fuzzy pink. We make a final adjustment to our packs, take a couple deep breaths, and walk into the cool, frothy canyon of the Stillwater.

The first few hundred yards of the Stillwater Trail is pinched to the river's edge by sheer walls of metamorphic rock. In early to mid-June snowmelt makes a hard run for the lowlands, the water roiling and bellowing with utter abandon, obliterating all sounds, giving those who walk this path the distinct feeling that they've crossed a kind of threshold into an especially vigorous, spirited place. From this point you could walk through more than sixty miles of wild country before crossing a single road, and after that one road, walk another forty before crossing another, a thought that strengthens my step and leaves me giddy at the same time.

Even with such a sensational port of entry, I fully expect it will take me several hours of walking before I can get my mind to stop chattering—to cease worrying about bills that need to be paid and calls that should be made and whether Abby the cat, who right now is trying to keep the home front safe from rodents, will be smart enough to stay clear of coyotes and foxes and the occasional stray dog looking to scare up a game of chase. But much to my relief, today I find that by the end of the first easy hour, the part of my brain in charge of anxious babble begins to relinquish control. Perhaps it's overwhelmed by the fancy dance of the river, by the soft, heady clusters of sticky geranium and wild rose, by the deep blue-green pools of the Stillwater, turning like slow dreams along the frothy edges of the main current.

We're little more than three miles up the trail when I'm jolted out of a rather pleasant stupor by the sound of rocks bouncing down the tall gray cliffs that flank the east side of the river. Uncapping the binoculars, I scan the upper ledges in time to catch sight of a snow-white nanny and kid mountain goat ambling along the edge of oblivion. The kid leaps, and slips on a loose rock. I catch my breath. She recovers quickly, though, and turns to watch loose stones tumble down two hundred stories of mountain. If she's moved at all, she doesn't show it. Despite the ingenious foot design of these animals, which consists of two spreadable toes underlain by extremely well-gripping traction pads, it stretches the imagination to see them dancing their dizzy pirouettes up and down these sheer, ledgeless walls. This is the ultimate no-net high-wire act, and it's performed regularly by goats as young as a week old. For so many thousands of years have mountain goats laid claim to the highest, most inaccessible reaches of the alpine world that their eyes have evolved to point downward. With the exception of the rare golden eagle daring enough to try to nab a young kid on the wing, there are no predators but for those who exist below.

The goats soon disappear over the lip of the precipice. We reposition our packs, looking for that increasingly hard-to-find adjustment that will make our loads comfortable again, and move on. The day is warming rapidly, fingers of sunlight working moisture out of the lush patches of bluebells and currants until the air hangs thick with the smell of earth and vegetation.

Within the hour we enter our first real patch of burned timber—the lower limits of the Storm Creek fire. Just as the hiker at the trailhead said, here are acres and acres of blackened tree trunks—slight, gaunt shadows of the former forest, knee deep in fields of fluttering wheatgrass, twisted stalk, fireweed, and spirea. On some trees the charred bark has split open to reveal striking slashes of smooth, beige- to alabaster-colored wood. Such splitting is a sign of a hot burn. Hot enough, in fact, to roast the millions of insects that typically live in a patch of forest like this one, and thus send the flickers and woodpeckers that feed on them winging off to more lucrative pickings someplace else.

These thick fields of grass are more than ample to provide good forage for wildlife. But the stripping of the forest by the fire has caused most animals to choose places well away from busy trails, away from the peering eyes of humans and their foul-smelling strings of horses and mules. We find elk tracks cast in the dry, gray dirt, but little more. We do catch occasional glimpses of mountain bluebirds, which sometimes nest in such burns, gathering their insect dinners on the wing. Red-tailed hawks are also easy to spot, hanging like kites on the late summer winds, scanning the open swales of brown grass for mice and voles.

At first I find the lower reaches of the Storm Creek burn to be interesting, but not really enthralling. The scene is, after all, like scenes from countless smaller fires that sizzle up and down the Rocky Mountains nearly every summer. The trail climbs easily across hummocks and in and out of small ravines studded with charred skeletons, offering us one slice of burn-scape after another, yet never really yielding a view of the entire pie. Thus for a time our feel for the fire grows not by miles, but by smaller increments—by feet and yards. The stories that one wrangler told me of trying to run a string of wild-eyed pack horses out of this canyon through waves of wind-driven smoke, angry flames exploding trees behind him like rounds of mortar in the thick of war, seem almost impossible to imagine.

But in another mile the trail begins a slow rise to the crest of a high ridge and, in one magnificent unveiling, exposes a fifteen-mile-long view of the rugged upper reaches of the Stillwater drainage. It is here that the Storm Creek burn slaps us in the face. The world before us—and it is a grand, yawning world of astonishing proportions—is utterly ravaged by fire. Two-thousand-foot reaches of mountain stand hard and bare, their tattered, wind-sheared cloaks of timber roasted and lying crumpled on the stone. It's as if these mountains have never felt the touch of green plants, as if they are freshly risen from the earth. I could easily believe that eons must pass before the first cracks will open in the rocks and catch the scattering of seeds, that centuries will spin before green and orange patches of lichen begin to massage the stone into tiny particles of soil. The scene is made even more penetrating by the fact that at the moment there is almost no sound—just a slight hiss from a small cascade of water plunging through the burn on the other side of the canyon. The effect of this silence is to heighten the dramatics of the landscape, like scenes from a movie where the sound is slowly bled away to increase the impact of the visual.

Of course these mountains aren't anywhere near being fresh out of creation, merely fresh out of a burn—a burn that has helped the land far more than hurt it. For one thing, burning (as opposed to logging) releases nutrients bound up in the trees and returns them to the soil; one study in Yellowstone National Park found that fireweed growing in an area burned during the 1988 fires was roughly 30 percent richer in nutrients than that growing elsewhere. Diseases are controlled through burn, and crowded timber stands, which sport little in the way of graze for wildlife, are thinned considerably. The truth is that the forest systems of the Rockies cannot maintain their health and vigor without the touch of flame; they have always been, and should always remain, a land created and recreated from the ashes.

Yet I am not spared occasional pangs of sadness at the overwhelming scope of this and other major burns of 1988. I've always clung to images of wildness in which change occurs within a framework of cold, clear streams and grand sweeps of forests reaching for the sky. To appreciate fires of this magnitude means learning to celebrate the small, initial movements of creation that most of us never give thought to—small pinches of fireweed or a lone daisy easing a tiny flush of green into the black of the burn. In such places wildness no longer seems so much a product as a process—a sluggish, persistent unfolding that will need two or three more centuries to run its course. I find it unsettling to hold my own lifetime up against the roll of a single mature conifer forest, and come up so terribly short.

In another hour we pass Wounded Man Creek, now nearly at the end of its wild, hell-bent run for the Stillwater. Though no one can tell me how this feisty little stream got its name, I find it interesting that there is another Wounded Man Creek close by, over the divide to the west. Was there in fact a wounded man—someone with a broken leg, or a crusty miner bleeding at the shoulder from the swipe of a grizzly paw— dragging himself up and down these forbidding ridges? Did he live to tell about it, to spin tales in some musty Virginia City bar, while his friends, thrilled by the entertainment, plunked down coins to keep him supplied in shots of warm rye?

Standing alongside the cascades of Wounded Man we can see occasional glimpses of sunlit waterfalls on the other side of the canyon, several of which are fed by remnant glaciers, lying thick and white like sheets of freezer ice atop the Stillwater Plateau. With no forest cover, the late-August heat is intense, so we opt for a skinny dip in the cold, clear waters of the creek. Frankly, I'm a little worried about how good it feels to take my pack off—that momentary sensation that gravity has been almost done away with, that but for the boots on my feet I might just float away. Taking a pack off shouldn't be quite such a relief this early in the day. What kind of shape will I be in this evening, I wonder, after eight more miles and fifteen hundred additional feet of climbing? Ah, but for now there is this sweet swell of water, and the sun is lying warm and heavy on our legs and faces. We munch for a while on cheese and crackers, and then lie back on the cool rocks, drifting away with the rush of the stream.

Locked in this afternoon stupor, I find myself thinking of Pat Quayle, a young man of twenty-four who in 1915 launched a remarkably unshackled ramble through the backcountry of Yellowstone. Quayle had spent the summer working for a concessionaire, catching fish from Shoshone Lake and the Madison River to serve the swarms of hungry tourists. When his job came to a close in September, he and another seasonal worker secured a couple of pack horses, loaded up with food, and set out walking with no particular agenda. After an initial trek that lasted well into early winter, Quayle returned in March to take on several hundred more miles. "We are vagabonds of a peculiar type," he writes in the first page of his diary. "Our chief pleasure is in roving about the mountains. Each of us has a month's wages—forty-five dollars—and consequently we feel wealthy. Our lives are free from care, therefore we have but to enjoy ourselves."

Reading Quayle's diary, I'm fascinated to see how his wanderings seemed to sink him deeper and deeper into musings about the importance of man's relationship to the earth.

Rarely did the sunlight break or a blizzard blow without rein-forcing a growing belief that nature, and not material goods, was the foundation of good living. "It is not surprising that Delacy, Stuart, Huston and others in their maddening search for gold paid little heed to geysers or canyon or lake. A fitting example of the effect upon the greater sense of man wielded by the lust for the filthy lucre. Valuable only as a means of exchange, yet used in such a way that it rules the earth—making tyrants of the rich and criminals of the poor . . . So long as these mountains remain for any appreciation I hope to live and die within the limits of necessity. Why should I store up wealth for a rainy day, when the trout bite best during the storm?"

By the end of our second day we reach the rich bottom lands of the upper Stillwater, where once again, thankfully, we find ourselves in cool, dark stands of living spruce and fir. Here the fires did little but nuzzle the base of the trees, char-ring them, leaving a forest where stout, tar-colored trunks rise out of a shaggy carpet of fireweed and crested wheatgrass. While it's a relief to be back in a green forest again, it brings to mind the fact that we're sharing this world of dark, ragged shadows with the great bear. When you're new to backpacking in grizzly country, as we are, strange things seem to happen in the waning hours of daylight. We glimpse charred stumps and rounded rock slabs out of the corners of our eyes and, like children in a dark bedroom, think we see movement there. At one point a large cow moose and calf step onto the trail well in front of us; in the fading, murky light there is that long, grinding second of squinting and searching, adrenaline spilling into our blood, while we try to fathom what it is we're really seeing.

Like most packers in grizzly country, Jane and I have adopted a code of conduct that we respect as if it had been delivered by a holy man on tablets of stone. We do not cook in or near the tent, and hang our food high in a tree every night. We leave no dirty dishes around until morning, nor do we sleep in the same clothes that we cooked in. Much as I love to eat fish I have left the fishing gear behind, paranoid that bears would pick trout smells off of me and our camp, come to investigate, and mistake me lying in my sleeping bag for a giant sushi roll. Part of this uneasiness is no doubt due to those images I saw as a kid of crazed, slobbering grizzlies on the covers of *Outdoor Life*. But the truth is that if bears were so inclined they could easily make mincemeat pie out of far more hikers and hunters than they do, instead of spending most of their days grubbing for biscuit root, yampa, and other salad fixings in the meadows of the backcountry. On average, only one person per year dies in North America at the claws of the grizzly; twelve times as many people die from bee stings, and fifty times that number perish each year from bolts of lightning.

Nevertheless, at this point, fresh on the heels of the evening shadows, we're hardly above employing grizzly-proofing techniques that are anchored more in superstition than common sense. Many a crusty old mountaineer I've met wouldn't think of bedding down for the night without first urinating around the camp. So every evening well before bedtime, Jane dutifully prompts me to begin drinking all the water, lemonade, or tea I can handle, so that by bedtime I'm ready and able to set about marking as much territory as my bladder will allow. (What a surprise that the quick side step I learned as a boy writing my name in the snow would come in so handy in protecting me from ferocious beasts of the forest.) Naturally, every morning that we wake up with no teethmarks on us is one more shred of proof that the ritual worked. In defending the practice, I'm reminded of the Hopi elder who was once asked if he'd ever, in the name of rational analysis, considered foregoing his dawn ritual of welcoming up the sun. The old man turned to the interviewer with steely eyes. "You would risk plunging the world into darkness for the sake of your stupid experiment?" In truth, the Hopi would never consider toying with the threads that connect him to the processes of his universe; likewise, I am certainly not ready to dull my dearly held presumption that I'm somehow sending news of great importance to the most powerful creature in America.

While my sense for the danger that grizzlies pose will

greatly diminish over time, my awareness of them will only grow deeper. As the miles of trail unfold I'll start drawing less on my fear of the bear and more on the layers of myth and magic that surround him. The Ancient Greeks considered bears to be no less than sculptors of human life and behavior— an attribute that may have originally come from watching mother bears lick their helpless, somewhat shapeless newborn cubs into a state of healthy response. Some folklorists claim that this notion rose again in the tale of Goldilocks. A little girl who stumbles into the home of a bear family and proceeds to try out various chairs, beds, and bowls of porridge, points to the reputation that bears once had for helping children forge their identities.

In early America, though, most positive bear myths (like many other myths of the day) got left behind on the shores of Europe. Here were bears not in symbol but in flesh, and they were soon equated with all that was loathsome about the wilderness. In a culture whose relationship to the cosmos was based on a fierce battle between ultimate good and ultimate evil, the bear was clearly a devil. It was no coincidence that for many people the first sense of really appreciating black bears came at Yellowstone, after we had used mounds of garbage to fashion them into a troupe of dump-side entertainers.

In the coming months the grizzly will offer me an invitation to see life from another perspective, one that says the greatest mysteries have qualities both wonderful and horrible. The fierce confusion of a blizzard, a lightning bolt jabbing at you from the crest of a high ridge, and perhaps most especially, the grizzly, are chances to get beyond a purely aesthetic relationship to the wilderness—to walk in a circular world, a world held together not by the tension of good and evil, but rather by the consent that life will always be at its most radiant when held fast against the calm, inevitable shadows of death.

TWO

An old Chinese proverb claims that it's not the thousand-mile journey that beats you, but rather the grain of sand in your shoe. For those who trudge through the wilds with backpacks on, it is not a grain of sand that proves to be the problem, but something as silly as a fold in a liner sock, or boots that haven't been properly broken in, or sweaty feet, or even the awkward, lumbering gait that unconsciously evolves as you hump your load higher and higher up the side of a mountain. We're talking blisters. And while blisters may have only slightly more conversational appeal than jock itch or yeast infections, they are truly the hiker's nightmare—those little red spots that, if untended, can grow into a gnawing, relentless source of pain, a pain that makes bears and bugs and weather seem like the most minor of distractions. Only fools and beginning backpackers who know no better head into the wilds without "moleskin," a closely woven flannel specifically designed to ease the rubbing of leather against skin.

So we were fools. But I had already put a good two thousand miles of walking on my boots, and Jane a good thousand miles, and neither of us had experienced a blister of any kind. So it comes as somewhat a surprise when Jane pulls her boot off at the end of our second day of hiking to find several of the dreaded red, tender spots lining her toes and heels. "Sweaty feet," she concludes, reading her blisters with the intensity of a fortune teller looking for answers in a wash of tea leaves. "I'll just have to air them out more often tomorrow." Already feeling like the village idiot for not packing the moleskin, I rummage around in my backpack, thinking that some shred of the stuff may have escaped my attention. But I have nothing to offer but Band-Aids and electrician's tape. The former will only cause more irritation; the latter, I'm quite sure, has seldom been tested for use on the body.

Early the next morning we continue our climb out of the Stillwater Canyon, the land now a patchwork of burn mingled with green, shaggy patches of towering spruce and fir. Jane's feet continue to worsen, but she says little about it, not calling for a break until nearly eleven o'clock. This time when she pulls her boots off I notice she's wincing with pain. When at last her liner socks have been carefully peeled away, we both sit in utter shock, Jane finally breaking into tears, and I into incredulous wincing curses. Large blisters have broken on the backs of her heels, and the constant climbing action—feet pressed hard against the back of the boots—has rubbed the tender layer of new skin underneath just short of the point of bleeding. Similar, smaller sores cover the bottoms of several toes, with one particularly angry-looking welt rising on the top of the second toe of her left foot. I have never seen anything like it. If the philosopher who said genius is the infinite capacity for taking pain was right, then Jane has already demonstrated clear brilliance. Unfortunately, I fear she'll need to be of near-wizard rank to manage the thirty miles of trail still ahead.

Desperate, I get out the electrician's tape, and we begin carefully building layers around the sides of the worst blisters, creating a doughnut of material for the shoes and socks to rub against. Then I unload some of her equipment into my pack, and we trudge on. Fortunately, this seems to afford some measure of relief.

In another two miles, after a steep climb along a small cascade of icy water, the trail breaks out into the grand sweep of meadows that make up Abundance Basin. Getting to this point on the Stillwater Trail is a passage of sorts; from here you can almost feel the heart of the Beartooths—in the pulse of water dancing past mats of phlox and forget-me-nots, in the rise of subalpine fir, in the sudden chill that creeps down from the high plateaus with the setting sun.

This is the Yellowstone Rockies in all their glory. Standing on the banks of the Stillwater—a river now small enough to step across—the world is a carnival of geology. Underfoot are coarse-grained slabs of gneiss, or "basement" rock, brewed in the hot belly of the earth more than 3 billion year ago. This is the misty stuff of the Precambrian Era, the last page in the scientific book of geological time, that point at which the landscape disappears into the fog altogether. The word *Cambrian* is a Latin derivative of an old Celtic word, *combroges*—literally, compatriots—a name once given to the people of Wales. If you were a Welshman in the 1500s, you were a "Camber" man, a title that sounds more distinguished than it really was.

In 1836, a geologist by the name of Sedgwick was poking around in the outback of Wales and Cumberland and came across an entirely new system of rocks, one which proved to be about 600 million years old. This was a good couple of hundred million years older than any previously known rock formation. But even more significant was the fact that in these folds would be found fossils of the very first animals on earth. Because of the region in which the discovery was made, the rocks were said to belong to the Cambrian period, or to be more precise, the Cambrian period of the Paleozoic Era. Geological history is broken down into eras, and each era further broken into periods. At the time Sedgwick made his discovery, the Paleozoic was the oldest era, and his Cambrian system became the oldest period within it. Since then much older rocks have been discovered, and an entirely new era was created to accommodate them, the Precambrian.

Long after the Precambrian rocks of the Beartooths were formed, and thick sheets of sediment had been laid on top of them by the comings and goings of various oceans, great colisions began to occur along several cracks, or faults, in the earth's crust. The pressure became so terrific that a great slice of earth bounded by those faults began inching into the sky. At their height the Beartooths may have reached a level fully four miles above sea level—a virtual ocean of mountains, most of them the height of Mount McKinley. Add a long period of erosion by wind, water, and—perhaps most important of all—three-thousand-foot-thick tongues of glacial ice licking out the granite valleys like they were so much ice cream, and you end up with the scene before us today.

Of course similar processes went on throughout much of the West. But the Beartooths are so broad and brazen, there's such a raw, rough-hewn feeling to them, that somehow their geology seems more immediate, more close to the touch. To stand in a shower of sunlight at the feet of these great peaks is to feel like you've made it to the cutting edge of creation. For just a split second my mind stops analyzing, stops comparing what I see to anything I've ever known before. This is all new. Every bit of it. And beneath the quiet, rugged veneer there seems to be the faintest thrum of life erupting—of life being, in Nietzsche's words, a great wheel rolling out of its own center.

Prospectors, either singly or in small groups, began searching this basin for gold well over a hundred years ago. And while they did cause a certain amount of damage to the environment, that damage was controlled not only by the limited scale of their tools, but by the place itself—the hard slap of winter, the threat of Indians, and always the rugged, unyielding terrain. Efforts to mine in the Abundance Basin were seriously complicated by grizzlies, who from this point west to Slough Creek just didn't seem to take kindly to intruders of any sort. In fact, for a party of five men in 1870, among the first to actually find gold at Lake Abundance, wildlife in general was more than a little bothersome.

Things began to get dicey in the middle of a quiet June night, when, as the men were peacefully snoozing in their camp just below Boulder Pass, a bull bison decided to issue a wake-up call by charging right through the middle of the tent. Having barely collected themselves from that encounter, the next afternoon another bison took aim at A. Bart Henderson, steamrolling right over the top of him, and was about to begin battering the pack horses when he was finally brought down by bullets from several rifles.

One would assume that by the time they reached Lake Abundance the party was more than ready for a little peace and quiet. But it was not to be. On July 9, Henderson and a prospector known only as "Dad" survived a terrific fight with a grizzly sow trailing three cubs, only to later that afternoon meet up with a ferocious male bear that Henderson claims weighed in at over nine hundred pounds. (By comparison, a large male grizzly in Yellowstone today weighs five hundred to six hundred pounds.) The next day Henderson's diary reports that the party met and killed six more bears. The day after that, Henderson was chased up a tree by an old female, which he eventually managed to shoot and kill from high in his piney perch.

In between arguments with the four-legged residents, the men did manage to make a decent gold strike near present-day Cooke City. Instead of working it then and there, though, they elected to put the job off until the following year and continue their tramp through the high country. Soon afterward the party was attacked by Indians while camping near Sunlight Creek. While no one was killed, every single horse was stolen, leaving the men with stocks of food, tools, blasting powder, and more than two dozen bearskins, but with no way to move any of it anywhere. Ever stalwart, the party cached their supplies and set off on foot to retrace their route back to Crow Agency, a long hundred miles of trail to the northeast.

Today's hunt for gold does not come and go with the scant impacts that it had when "Dad" and A. Bart Henderson roamed these highlands. Very near where we now stand, just two miles from Yellowstone Park and even less from the Absaroka-Beartooth Wilderness, the Canadian-based Noranda Corporation is planning one of the largest gold mining operations in the region. Of the countless projects currently slated for the Yellowstone ecosystem, from clear-cuts to oil drilling to condos, it would be hard to name one with greater potential impact than Noranda's New World Mine. For the twelve- to fifteen-year life of the operation, 140 people will unearth 1,200 to 1,800 tons of ore each day from a complex web of underground tunnels and cavities. The silver and copper will be reduced to concentrate and then shipped to a smelter, possibly in Canada. Gold, on the other hand, was originally to be collected on-site using cyanide, a fairly typical method of extraction when working with low grade surface deposits. When it was later discovered that the bulk of the gold was actually contained in high-grade underground reserves, plans for the cyanide leaching system were abandoned. Of course it's still possible, even likely, that a cyanide system will be put into place once the underground reserves are exhausted.

Covering two thousand acres, the mine will be in close proximity to the headwaters of the three major tributaries of the Yellowstone River: Miller Creek, which flows into Yellowstone Park via Soda Butte Creek; the Clarks Fork River via Fisher Creek (the Clarks Fork, incidentally, is the only Wild and Scenic River in the entire state of Wyoming); and the pristine Stillwater, by way of Daisy Creek. As noted earlier, the Stillwater will also be receiving additional pollution if the state grants water quality exemptions to the Stillwater Mine, located twenty-five miles downstream.

Even with the utmost care, the chance of water degradation here is extreme. For one thing, snowfall in the Fisher Creek drainage, where the mill and a 5.5 million-ton tailings impoundment are likely to be located, is remarkably high—typically twenty-five to forty feet per year. During periods of rapid melt or heavy early spring rains it's questionable whether the tailings impoundment will be capable of containing the release; if not, toxic waters could be loosed into the Wild and Scenic Clarks Fork River. To make matters worse, the Fisher Creek drainage is riddled with some of the most formidable avalanche paths in the state.

I might feel better if this or similar operations already underway weren't being run on such a fervent profit-or-die mentality. The Montana Hard Rock Mining Bureau, which is hardly a junkyard dog when it comes to protecting resources, has already had to shut down Noranda's Montanore mine south of Libby, Montana; for a full year and a half during the exploration phase, the company polluted local streams with nitrate levels that in some months ran as much as seventeen times permissible standards. Ever quick to reassure, the project's mine manager described the offense as a "technical" violation. Similarly, when it came time for Noranda's New World Mine to establish baseline data for water runoff in Fisher Creek Drainage, the company initially chose a ten-year cycle marked by the worst drought conditions in decades. In most places, of course, you can't even build a house without first establishing that it will lie outside the hundred-year floodplain.

Reclamation could prove to be another problem. Last year I toured the mine site with a Noranda geologist—an amicable, well-seasoned fellow, with eyes that beamed whenever the conversation drifted toward the intricacies of the mining process. But he was obviously less at ease when it came to massaging the ice out of controversial issues dealing with long-term consequences to the environment. Much of the time he would offer vague assurances, claim that he really wasn't the person to address the issue, or else remind us that we'd soon be seeing a fine example of mine reclamation, playing the promise like a wild card in a game of high-stakes poker. Standing beside the geologist, obviously relieved each time trouble was defused, was the mine security guard—a somber, brick warehouse of a man in a brown leather vest and a cowboy hat, fresh in from the gold mines of Nevada.

The reclamation site the geologist kept referring to was at the old McLaren Mine, a ragged slew of fifty-year-old toxic rubble strewn across the face of Fisher Mountain. The Forest Service has been working off and on with this reclamation project for over sixteen years, yet what I saw was hardly anything to bring hope to the heart. While heavy fertilization had allowed native plant stock to begin taking hold on level ground, the sloped plots looked pathetic—sparse clusters of tiny, forlorn plants, struggling against an almost constant barrage of acidic runoff. When I asked about the lack of successful reclamation on the slopes, the geologist's eyes went steely again, and the security guard stiffened. "We're confident we'll leave the area better than it's been in fifty years," he said—a vague reference not to Noranda's ability to reclaim alpine slopes (no one has managed that very well), but to the fact that the company will probably be required to clean up the noxious clutter left by the McLaren brothers as a condition of their permit to mine. Whether they can in fact do that is questionable. (Recently, when a company geologist was questioned about severe soil erosion at a roadside test drill site, he simply shrugged and explained that his boss had told him "not to worry about it.")

In 1969, at another site further downstream, Kennecott Copper leveled and shaped mill tailings, covered them with two to four feet of topsoil, and rerouted Soda Butte Creek around the debris. Yet when scientists sampled the creek a year and a half later, the water had almost exactly the same levels of pollutants it did before reclamation. Four years later, a researcher under contract with the National Park Service retested the site (remember, this creek dumps into Yellowstone Park), and made the following conclusions: "The seepage from the mill tailings is adversely affecting the water quality of Soda Butte Creek. The natural flora and fauna present above the tailings were either eliminated or severely reduced immediately below the tailings. Algae were eliminated . . . and other aquatic flora was not observed. The macroinvertebrates were considerably reduced in both numbers and diversity and on several occasions were entirely absent. Fish were not present and bioassays showed the stream to be highly toxic to fingerling trout." In other words, despite significant reclamation efforts by Kennecott, the stretch of Soda Butte Creek immediately below the tailings was, and continues to be to this day, a dead stream.

Even if Noranda's initial reclamation efforts were as successful as the geologist had suggested, it would hardly be indicative of the future condition of the site. Dr. Kenneth

Pierce is an award-winning geologist from Yale who has worked for twenty-five years on surface geological processes in the Yellowstone area. He says that erosion of fully stabilized and reclaimed tailings piles occurs from several natural processes, any of which can result in toxic material being carried into nearby streams. Rapid snowmelt or rain falling onto melting snow, for instance, can easily cut gullies into stored tailings. (High mountain terrain, as you might imagine, is especially vulnerable to all types of erosion.) Similarly, fire can move through and burn away the protective cover vegetation, again leading to exposure of the tailings. Extreme wetting of the soil can cause large surface movements called slumping; the clay that will probably be used to cap the tailings of the New World Mine is quite vulnerable to such movement. The bottom line is that to ensure downstream water quality, monitoring and maintenance of tailings piles will have to go on not for decades, but for centuries. "To assume basic reclamation solves the problem," says Pierce, "is like saying the original paint and roofing on a new house will permanently protect it."

Despite the fact that 4 billion dollars' worth of minerals are taken from federal lands each year, under the existing 1872 mining law, not a single penny of royalties is paid to the government. Furthermore, when someone locates minerals on federal lands they can then "patent" the claims, which in many cases tranfers the land to private ownership at a cost to the mining company of roughly two and a half to five dollars per acre. So far, more than 3 million acres of public land (about five thousand square miles) have fallen into private hands. Sometimes the land is then resold to developers for hundreds of times the cost of the original investment; in one case on the Oregon coast, slightly less than eight hundred acres of land patented for under two thousand dollars is now worth 12 million dollars.

Whatever monies state and federal agenices have for stabilization projects come from reclamation bonds set up before actual mining begins. Unfortunately, in many cases these bonds aren't enough to ensure adequate reclamation in the first place, let alone allow for long-term care of the mined area. Several experts have suggested that Noranda be required to fund a sizable endowment, so that long after the company has abandoned the region monies will still be available to deal with the inevitable task of long-term maintenance and monitoring. If such financial precautions are not taken, and right now there is little hope that they will be, the cost of cleanup will once again fall on the heads of the taxpayers. According to the Western Interstate Energy Board, the current price tag for cleaning up abandoned and inactive mines just in the state of Montana is a staggering 912 million dollars. There are currently over a thousand abandoned hardrock mines in the greater Yellowstone area alone.

The list of impacts from this project goes on and on, from the loss of grizzly habitat to the construction of a sixty-eight-mile-long power line corridor in one of only two relatively undeveloped drainages remaining in the Yellowstone ecosystem; from operating lights that will be visible to hikers from peaks throughout the Beartooths to potential loss of recreation dollars to nearby Cooke City. But what's really amazing is the way in which those locals trying to act as watchdogs of this project are being treated by pro-mine factions—ways that seem only a few shades removed from the brutal days of early Butte, when henchmen for the mines kidnapped union leaders and hanged them from railroad trestles.

Wade King is chairman of the Beartooth Alliance, a grass-roots citizens' group of two hundred members devoted not so much to stopping the mine as to holding it accountable for its actions. King tells of being in a bar in Cooke City last year, when a Noranda contractor angry with his views came up behind him and knocked him unconscious. Despite earlier assurances by Noranda that such behavior would be cause for immediate dismissal, the project manager claimed that the matter was simply a personal difference of opinion between King and the contractor, completely unrelated to the mine. Soon thereafter the company purchased the place King was renting and evicted him; when I spoke to him later in the summer, he was living in a tent. A few weeks later, someone placed a call to the Park County sheriff's department, alleging that they had seen King selling drugs outside a local bar. Shortly after the incident, obviously still shaken, Wade told me he expected more violence to be directed at the Alliance in the future, and at the leadership in particular. "If they expect to get rid of me, they're going to have to eliminate me from the planet"—a possibility that, by the sober look on his face, he had not ruled out entirely. Dramatic polarization of the community continues to this day, a situation often exacerbated by Noranda itself. For instance, the company continues to tell its employees to patronize only "acceptable" local businesses—in other words, those with owners who clearly support the mine.

For years recreation has accounted for over 80 percent of all public lands-related jobs in the greater Yellowstone area, contributing roughly 200 million dollars annually to local economies. Mineral development, on the other hand, accounts for less than 3 percent of employment, and contributes under 4 percent of the total revenues. Given this fact, the use of scare tactics might be seen as a desperate attempt to keep the road open for future mining development. Another far more successful technique consists of promising the locals the moon when your company first comes into an area, and then once you have their support, start backing for the door.

"When Noranda first came into Cooke City," says Wade King, "they went through the usual ritual of passing out trinkets. They bought a new computer for the school, and put a new light on the fire hall." Residents pressed Noranda officials to help protect their recreation-based economy, and the company said it was behind them all the way, tossing out suggestions for a corporate-funded city park, a network of hiking, snowmobile, and ski trails, even a civic center. But when the proposed plan of operation came out, the only offering was to extend a single existing snowmobile trail—an addition that the local snowmobile club rejected years earlier because snowslides made the route too hazardous.

"You need to understand that we're not against mining," King says of the Beartooth Alliance. "The Jardine Mine near

Gardiner is a great example of how a company can work hand in hand with a community to knock down road blocks ahead of time. But Noranda's basic position has been 'make us do it or we're not going to do it.' They see anyone who doesn't believe in total, unregulated extraction as the enemy." Sadly, this kind of approach, predicated on deception and lack of concern for social and environmental values, has for many extractive companies become standard operating procedure. Along with wholesale oil and gas leasing and unsustainable timber cuts on the national forests, it is part of an astonishing, haunting legacy of abuse.

As day fades to darkness, and we finally crawl into our sleeping bags along the north shore of Lake Abundance, I find myself thinking less of mining than of the trials and tribulations of the Henderson party. Such fantasy proves unfortunate, because when Jane jabs me later and tells me that there's something very big roaming around right outside the tent, I already have some pretty potent images of "Dad" and Mr. Henderson locked in a fierce struggle against hordes of grizzly commandos in this very basin. As I listen to the noise outside the tent growing ever louder—the kind of listening where you find yourself straining so hard that you forget to breathe—I'm quite sure that it's an animal with hooves instead of padded feet. That, and the fact I've been told a dozen times that I'd definitely know a grizzly when I heard it, gives me the courage to rise slowly up on my elbow and shine a light into the blackness. There, not ten feet away from me, is the homely yet remarkably welcome face of a bull Shiras moose. After turning toward me and blinking a few times, the two of us trading curious stares across the thin beam of light, he looks away, snorts softly, and strolls off into the woods, leaving Jane and me lying in the tent pushing out long sighs of relief.

From what little I could see of our caller he looked to be about six feet high at the shoulder, and I would guess weighed somewhere in the neighborhood of eight hundred to nine hundred pounds. While that's certainly impressive—about the size of a horse—it is, incredibly, a good foot shorter and five hundred to six hundred pounds lighter than his cousins to the north in Alaska. Like all mature fall bulls, this fellow's huge, palmate antlers, which were five months in the making, have turned his long, plain face into something almost regal. There was no velvet on the antlers, a sign that the time is fast approaching when this fellow will begin that ancient autumn wildlife ritual, the rut—a vigorous sparring with other bulls for territory and mates. At that time he'll be a serious force to reckon with; a few hikers I've met say they worry less about being injured by grizzlies in the backcountry than by moose—particularly cows with calves, or bulls in rut.

Curiously, some of the bulls this moose will challenge may be the same companions he's just spent the past three or four months with, feeding and resting in relatively peaceful seclusion. Though the matches of the rut are not fights to the death, there is always the possibility of injury. There have been cases of bull moose going at each other with such ferocity that their antlers actually become locked, a situation that sometimes leads to a slow, sorry death for both animals.

The gangly appearance of moose, especially those without a spread of antlers to bring them a much-needed dose of the horizontal, belies an absolute genius of design. The existence of strangely jointed legs allows the animal to navigate deep snow, and also to pull itself free from the draw of muddy stream bottoms where it so often feeds. Similarly, a part of each hoof known as the dew claw spreads wide each time the moose puts weight on it, buoying him in soft mud much the way a snowshoe holds a person up on soft snow. Moose will not only feed in water above their heads, but have been spotted in lakes acting like gangly pearl divers, plunging fifteen or twenty feet to the bottom to nab mouthfuls of aquatic plants. They're superb swimmers, able to cross open waters like the nine-mile-wide Grand Manan Channel off the coast of Maine at an impressive clip. No wonder the myths of many early Northeast peoples talk of moose as having been transformed from whales.

Over the five hundred miles that I walked through the Yellowstone Rockies, the moose became an extremely important animal to me, a creature that I saw on nearly every leg of my journey, and that in some strange way always left me strengthened, feeling somehow connected to the animal in a way that was far beyond any explanation of relationship offered by my own culture. Once, when I was sick with the flu hiking in the southwest corner of Yellowstone National Park, a moose showed up and for some bizarre reason I immediately felt better. Those times when I stumbled into camp beat and burned out from a long, hot day, as often as not there would be a moose there to greet me. The mornings that I started out just not feeling up to the long, exhausting day ahead, a moose would suddenly appear, and my spirits would soar.

I have no explanation for this. Quite frankly, while I've always been thrilled at seeing moose, if it were left to me to choose a "totem" animal for myself I probably would have picked something more sexy, like an eagle or a bear or a mountain lion. Then again, the moose does have a rather intriguing history.

To early Europeans in the remote regions of New England and Canada the moose was a critical source of food, having saved many a colonist and Jesuit missionary from starvation. In the seventeenth century both the English and the French had great plans to domesticate moose. Writing in 1634, Englishman William Woods considered the moose a perfect stock animal, "first because they are so fruitful, bringing forth three at a time," and also "because they will live in winter without any fodder." As for the French, in 1636 the Governor of Quebec somehow managed to wrangle a cow moose and two bulls into an enclosure, which was the first step in his plan to train them as pack animals for priests to use on their long, arduous journeys to the distant missions. Evidently the moose thought otherwise, though, as the reporter of this particular experiment, Friar Le Jeune, never mentioned the scheme in his writings again.

According to Algonquin myth, when the great god Glooskap first created man and all the creatures, the moose was enormous, taller than the tallest trees. When Glooskap realized that the moose was so big and strong that the people would never be able to kill it for food and clothing, he decided to make a slight alteration. The humped back, short body and bulging nose you see on the moose today are due to Glooskap having used his bare hands to squeeze the creature down to its present size.

One of my favorite stories about the moose comes from a tribe of people once known only as the Dog-Ribs, who live roughly three hundred miles south of the Arctic Circle, between the Great Bear and Great Slave lakes. Long ago, west of the Mackenzie River, there was a fierce giant named Naba-Cha. To give you a sense of how big this guy was, his lodge was covered with three hundred caribou skins, and each day he ate two caribou, a whole moose, or fifty partridges. For a slave the giant had a young Cree boy by the name of Ithenhiela, whom he'd stolen from the lands lying far to the south.

One day Hottah the moose felt sorry for the abused boy, and told him of a land far to the west, near the Yukon River, where there lived a great man who would protect him from the giant. Following Hottah's instructions, the boy collected a stone, a clod of earth, a piece of moss, and a branch of a tree. He then climbed on the moose's back, and together they headed west across the plains.

When the giant found his slave had escaped, he was furious, and wasted no time mounting his huge caribou to chase him down. "Throw down the clod of earth!" cried Hottah to the boy as the giant neared. When he did, great hills rose behind them, which slowed the giant down considerably. When next the giant started closing in Hottah told the boy to fling the moss, and when he did a huge muskeg swamp opened up, halting the giant's progress once again. When yet again the giant was almost upon them the boy was told to throw down the stone. At that point the Rocky Mountains began to rise, pushing into the northern sky until they touched the clouds. Many days later, after the giant had finally managed to cross the mountains, the boy was forced to throw down the branch, which created a vast, impenetrable forest through which the giant's caribou, with his enormous antlers, could not pass.

By this time the boy and Hottah the moose had managed to cross the Yukon. The giant finally staggered up to the other shore and begged Hottah to take him across, swearing that he would do no harm to the boy. Hottah returned for the giant, but in midstream threw him from his back, and he was swept into the rapids and drowned. And thus ended another adventure for Hottah the two-year-old moose, the "cleverest of all northern animals."

Many native peoples of the Northeast said that a person could travel several times farther on a meal of moose than on any other food. Furthermore, they assigned the animal great reasoning power. Thus they would never give moose meat to the dogs, lest the moose should discover this and conceal themselves from the hunters. Oddly, both Native Americans and Europeans—apparently independently of one another—believed that moose were subject to epilepsy, and could cure themselves by scratching an ear with the left hind foot until it drew blood. Thus in the late Middle Ages, both the most prominent doctors in Europe and the best medicine men of the Algonquin Indians were instructing epileptics to hold a moose hoof in their left hand and rub their ear with it. All in all, though, given my strange attraction to these great creatures, the belief I hang my hopes on most is one from the woods of Quebec, related in 1637 by the Jesuit emissary of Louis XV. "The Indians look upon the moose as an animal of good omen, and believe that those who dream of them often may expect a long life."

I find it sad that I don't really know what to do with my pull to the moose. I can admire him, but because the religion and philosophy of my people don't deal with such things, I cannot interpret him. And so there remains a hole in my life, a yearning fastened to a kernel of wonder, and me without the symbols to ever understand.

THREE

This first morning of September sparkles like cut glass. Sunlight is dancing hard on the ripples of Lake Abundance, while the thick buzz of mountain chickadees and the flutey, spiral songs of the hermit thrush spill out from the shadows of the spruce fir forest. It's that "magnificent fierce" morning that D. H. Lawrence spoke of finding, when you spring awake and the old world vanishes against the lightness of something entirely different and new. To me mornings in the backcountry are in general far more full of possibility than those that creep into the rooms of my house. Opening my eyes in places like this is close to the feeling I had as a kid waking on the first day of spring break. I suppose the biggest difference is that at thirty-five, I can no longer let myself sleep until ten o'clock; now a sunny day brings with it a slight sense of urgency, a feeling that here is something I can't afford to waste.

At nine o'clock two friends join us, having hiked in from a high ridge three miles to the southeast, near Daisy Pass. Their faithful Volkswagen van, veteran of many a Rocky Mountain road, lies floundered on a steep grade, but they're reconciled to the fact that rescue will have to wait until we get off the trail. With them is Luna the wonder dog, a cheery, good-natured black Lab that carries her own food on her back in a specially designed canvas pack. Luna is obviously ecstatic to be out and about like this, though I can't help but wonder if she'll miss the garbage cans that she occasionally turns to for long nights of unfettered feasting, returning home in the morning like an addict back from a binge, a shamed look smeared across the black of her face.

Thankfully, Nancy has brought moleskin, so Jane immediately begins doctoring her expanding blister collection. Last night her feet were so sore that she attached her rubber camp slippers not by pulling them on, but by folding down the sides and holding them against the bottom of her feet with rubber bands. We further divide her weight—eventually, even Luna will carry a couple of items—and head off to the west through another slice of burn, this time bound for the long, grassy reaches of Slough Creek.

Sometimes when I'm hiking I have a tendency to slip into a kind of hypnotic trance, my feet beating like the clicks of a metronome, until I find myself staring at the trail through glassy eyes, completely oblivious to whatever beauty or intrigue surrounds me. I'm in just such a state of numbness when out of the corner of my eye I see a flash of wing, and turn to see a magnificent great horned owl lunging from a branch not eight feet from my head. He doesn't go very far, and after situating himself on another perch, commences to stare at us with one of those supremely detached looks that only owls and certain behavioral psychologists can muster. This particular burn has been good to him, turning the land into a thick quilt of grasses spiked with hundreds of blackened perches—a utopia for any creature that makes much of its living hunting ground-hugging, grass-eating rodents. (Had this area been severely burned, however, this owl would've had to wait a good two years before rodent populations recovered.) Striking an imperial pose from a low branch of an Engelmann spruce, this chap reminds me of a comment made by a naturalist in New Hampshire, who said it seemed to him that owls were the masters of the woods, "and all the other birds mere satellites."

We're not the only culture to have toyed with the notion that owls possess a certain wisdom. The Blackfeet believe these birds are the spirits of great medicine men, while the Gros Ventre say that owls visit certain leaders in their dreams, offering them wise counsel, or even warning them of impending tragedy. Likewise, I can recall hearing old tales in the Midwest about the hoot of an owl being a portent of death; the Gros Ventre were plugged into nearly the same notion, saying that if an owl landed on the tent or house, or hooted from a nearby bush, someone in the tribe was about to die. Unlike our culture, however, which for a time abandoned the secrets and intrigue surrounding great horned owls and took to shooting them instead (they were considered ruthless killers), most Native American peoples never lost either their sense of mystery or reverence for these great birds.

Naturalist Robert McConnell Hatch once told of an owl "clucking, cackling, and snarling" directly over his camp. Looking for him each night with a flashlight, Hatch confessed to having "an uneasy suspicion that I was affording him a summer's entertainment." The Gros Ventre would have agreed. Owls love to play such games, explained one member of the tribe to an inquisitive anthropologist in the early 1950s. "They bother people and mock you when you talk or laugh."

By midafternoon we descend into the upper reaches of Slough Creek. Even though the timbered hills on both sides of the valley are badly burned, it does little to diminish the magic of the place. An immense span of meadow spills southward as far as we can see. Long waves of knee-high, honey-colored grass ripples in the early autumn sun, the valley cut roughly in half by a meandering line of willow rising from the banks of Slough Creek. Though at this point we're in the Gallatin National Forest, such landscapes are fairly typical throughout much of Yellowstone Park. They are not flashy or startling. They do not reach out and jolt you into a state of utter astonishment, as do the ramparts of the Tetons or the Absarokas. Yet leaving the highway and walking through these vast, seemingly limitless swales of pine and grass provokes a kind of passionate serenity that I have known in few other places. It is a heartland without boundaries, a wilderness that one does not so much penetrate as slip into, easing through the sights and smells of the highlands as one might slide into flannel sheets at the end of a cold December day.

A hundred and fifty years ago, that great trapper and man of consummate wanderlust, Osborne Russell, was moved by this area nearly to mush. Recalling his time spent in the Lamar River Valley, just fifteen miles south of where we now stand, Russell abandons his typical matter-of-fact prose and begins to wax poetic. "I almost wished I could spend the remainder of my days in a place like this, where happiness and contentment seemed to reign in wild romantic splendor, surrounded by majestic battlements which seemed to support the heavens and shut out all hostile intruders."

It was along the Lamar that Russell came upon a small band of the now-extinct Sheepeater Indians. Many nine-teenth-century authors have painted the Sheepeaters to be poor (primarily defined as a lack of horses), unskilled, wretched people living in the most squalid conditions, afraid of their own shadows—as one explorer put it, utterly "worthy of pity." Yet Russell, who has something of a reputation for honest reporting, sees a much different people. "They were all neatly clothed in dressed deer and sheep skins of the best quality," he writes, "and seemed to be perfectly contented and happy. They were well armed with bows and arrows pointed with obsidian. The bows were beautifully wrought from sheep, buffalo and elk horns secured with deer and elk sinews and ornamented with porcupine quills. We obtained a large number of elk, deer, and sheep skins from them of the finest quality, and three large neatly dressed panther skins in return for awls, adzes, kettles, tobacco, ammunition, etc. They would throw the skins at our feet and say 'give us whatever you please for them and we are satisfied. We can get plenty of skins, but we do not often see the Tibuboes' " (white people, or literally, people of the sun).

When I read passages from Russell's diary I get the sense that he appreciated this land, that he honestly enjoyed the simple ebb and flow of life. In this he stands in stark contrast to those men who swept through the forests and valleys of the Rockies primarily because there were no margins here to limit their swashbuckling ways. Men like Frenchy Durant, whose cabin stood just a few hundred yards north of us until it was finally swallowed by the fires of 1988. In fact, this long reach of grassland is still known to many as Frenchy's Meadows. Born the member of a prominent French Canadian family on a cold December day in 1861, as a young man Frenchy drifted southward out of Canada to the east face of the Beartooths, where he staked a gold claim. When the gold petered out he made a career shift, putting his hunting and trapping skills to work as a food supplier to the army garrison stationed at Fort Yellowstone. Some years later he tired of that too, and quit the chow business to hunt, fish, and, according to his wife, build nearly forty miles of road along the Cooke City Trail and into his home site here on Slough Creek.

As I've suggested, the stretch of land from Slough Creek to the Abundance Basin has long been a home for grizzlies, and for some reason Frenchy, who was brave to the point of being foolish, decided that it was his beck and call to do battle with the lord of the beasts. In his twenty or so years here on Slough Creek he is reported to have killed more than two hundred grizzlies, and to have captured another six in metal spring traps. It was the seventh of those trapped bears, a male of tremendous stature and power, that put an abrupt end to Frenchy's war. Having discovered the grizzly one morning while out for a walk, the steel jaws of the trap firmly clasped around the bear's leg, Frenchy hurried home to grab his skinning knife. As the day wore on and he didn't return his wife Jennie became concerned, and went out to look for him. But he was nowhere to be found. Fearing the worst, Jennie put in a call for help to the Yellowstone rangers.

When the rangers finally found old Frenchy, he was a good two miles from the site of an incredible struggle, his clothes completely torn off, his entire body so cut and mangled that the searchers decided to bury it on the spot. From what they could deduce, Frenchy had evidently fired one shot into the trapped grizzly, but the bullet missed its mark, only wounding the bear. At that point the old bruin became so enraged that he broke the chain and came after Frenchy in a fury that would be hard for most of us to imagine in our wildest nightmares, biting and clawing him, even smashing his rifle to bits, finally leaving him for dead. By some miracle Frenchy came to, and broken and bleeding, began crawling toward home. The fact that he survived two miles is strong testimony to how tough he really was. "I always knew Frenchy would die this way," said one of his friends. "He was too brave, too fearless, too strong, and too sure."

The notion that the old bruin was giving Frenchy eight hundred pounds of payback for all the killing he'd done to his fellow bears is just too tempting of a legend not to play with. Indeed, seventy years later, strange tales of Frenchy Durant and his bad karma with the big bears still float through the region. More than one person assured me that for years after Frenchy was dead and buried grizzlies were stopping by to pull him from the earth and scatter his bones through the meadows. At one point, a large iron fence was supposedly constructed around the grave site, but the bears demolished it as easily as Frenchy's killer snapped the links of that steel trap. Another local claimed that to this day grass has never grown on the grave site.

There is some evidence that the grizzlies of Slough Creek are still not winning any medals for hospitality. On a late summer night here ten years ago, a friend from Red Lodge had a close encounter with what he calls "the grizzly from hell." When the bear got a whiff of some fish that was cooking (admittedly, a poor choice of entrées), it began snarling and circling ever closer, finally causing the guy to hunker so near to his roaring campfire that he burned the eyebrows right off his face.

The sky tonight is riddled with stars, there are friends around the cook stove, and Slough Creek is humming the catchiest of tunes on its long shuffle toward the Lamar. Jim surprises us by bringing out a bottle of Jose Cuervo, and with a little salt and lime it actually tastes wonderful—never a good sign when drinking tequila. Unfortunately, I overindulge, and end up greeting the dawn on my knees in the willow thickets, dutifully swearing that I will never touch the golden bomb again. ("I saw you over there on your knees," Jim tells me later. "Hell, I thought you were meditating!") Unable to eat, I stretch out on a gravel bar on the edge of Slough Creek, sunlight full on my face and the calls of sandhill cranes floating overhead. When I finally don my pack I'm barely running on one cylinder, and the thought of walking fourteen miles in eighty-degree weather has about as much appeal as two tickets to a Muzak festival. With Jane's blisters forcing her to move as if she were walking over hot coals, and me looking like something a bear might drag out of a snowbank during the spring thaw, we trudge slowly on to the south, well behind Jim and Nancy.

Three miles out we pass the beautiful Silver Tip Guest Ranch, which would not be here at all were it not for some incredible firefighting heroics in 1988, when a powerful fire was finally halted on the very edge of the grounds. This beautiful place was first acquired in 1913 as a homestead property. But in 1922, two of the powerful East Coast Morgan Partners happened to hear of the Silver Tip during one of their western excursions, liked what they saw, and decided to buy it. (S. R. Guggenheim also ended up with a one-third interest in the Silver Tip, though he never set foot on it.) As it happened, the Morgan boys came along very soon after Frenchy Durant met his end at the paws of that trapped bear, so they decided to pay a visit to Frenchy's widow to see if she too was interested in selling off her holdings. Evidently the good widow Durant was out of Lafit Rothschild at the time, so instead she plied the House of Morgan with generous draughts of her home-made dandelion wine. It must have been good stuff: Jennie sold not only her land to the men, but nineteen head of cattle, two old horses, various old pieces of furniture, a stove, cooking utensils, and a strange array of rusty, useless diving equipment that Frenchy had picked up somewhere along the way.

Reading tales of Silver Tip visits during the twenties, thirties, and early forties brings a welcome splash of character to people with names like Rockefeller, Goodyear, Bliss, Hamilton, and Cushing. Most of the guests loved to fish, and reached their favorite angling pools either by horseback, or sometimes by driving one of several dilapidated vehicles, including a sorry-looking White truck that had no brakes. Once, when mice started nesting in the rear of one of the ranch cars—this one a faded green Buick—one of the guests took care of the problem by backing the car into a ford on Slough Creek until the rear seat was completely submerged, forcing the mice to abandon ship. When Neal Bliss took several friends on a tour of the park in the summer of 1923, the weather suddenly turned so cold that when one of the children peed in his pajamas, they froze stiff.

One gets the sense that despite the high level of wealth and social stature gathered under this roof, there was remarkably little pretension, as if the out-of-doors really was the great leveler that some have portrayed it to be. "Silver Tip might not do for everyone," wrote one of the regulars. "There are no singing cowboys, no fake round-ups, no fat-bottomed dude girls, no camp fires, camp mothers or entertainers. Fishing brings you home bone weary. The horses wander and must be found. There is haying to be done, wood cut." After a visit to Silver Tip with his wife, John D. Rockefeller went so far as to say that it was one of the most delightful experiences of his life.

Given Jane's and my sluggish pace, at twelve miles out Jim and Nancy decide to make a quick sprint to the trailhead, drive our vehicle back to Daisy Pass and pull out the Volkswagen, and then return to Slough Creek. Looking at us, they seem convinced we'll still be on the trail when they return— and at this point I have to agree—so before taking off they make additional plans to hike back up to meet us. An hour or so after they've left, the manager of the Silver Tip drives by in a horse-drawn wagon, brings it to a halt beside us, and asks if we're the "two people dying on the trail."

Of course we have no choice but to plod on, and by seven miles I'm starting to get a bit of an appetite back, and Jane has either deadened the nerves in her feet entirely or achieved sufficient genius over pain to carry on for a mile or two at a time without too much discomfort. Fortunately there are no steep climbs or descents, just an easy freefall down a long, sweet valley. To the west rises the grassy scarp of Buffalo Plateau, named by the same A. Bart Henderson who had so much trouble with grizzlies in Abundance Basin. Henderson notes that when his party came through in 1870, there were thousands of buffalo quietly grazing on it, a sight that my modern eyes would find heaven sent.

Another, even more intriguing high line rises to the south, past the point where Slough Creek joins forces with the Lamar. This is Specimen Ridge, and it's here that you'll find twenty-five square miles of the world's most famous petrified forests. The ridge is thick with the stony trunks of five-hundred-year-old trees, many still standing fully upright like the pillars of some ancient city, now all but buried in rubble. There are also pieces of trunk and branches scattered about the ground, as well as the spidery sprawl of root systems. And that's just the beginning. Twenty-seven separate forests lie here, one on top of the other, buried over the course of twenty thousand years in turbulent explosions of volcanic ash, dust, and lava; to reach the oldest of these prehistoric woodlands would require digging through twelve hundred feet of debris.

The kinds of fossilized trees and plants found here speak of a Yellowstone of 50 million years ago—one far different from what we know today. These were not cool temperate forests, marked by trees like Engelmann spruce, subalpine fir, and lodgepole pine. Instead there were dense weaves of sycamore, walnut, myrtle, magnolia, laurel, and chestnut; oak, redwood, persimmon, hickory, elm, ironwood, and bayberry. It was a subtropical place, where each year fifty or sixty inches of rain spilled from a warm sky onto wide lowland valleys and gentle mountains, the roll of the land as soft as the crumples in a bedsheet.

Of course none of us will live to see the kinds of biological shifts that are represented in the layers of Specimen Ridge. Yet it's not so farfetched to think that we might see a resurgence of the same volcanic activity that buried these hardwood forests in the first place. Because this portion of the earth's crust has been sliding slowly to the west, the large "hot spot" that was beneath Idaho's Snake River Plain millions of years ago is today found under Yellowstone Park; in fact, in the general vicinity of Yellowstone Lake there appears to be a large, potent magma chamber lying a scant one or two miles below the surface of the earth. In some geyser basins the amount of heat being given off is now a thousand times greater than what you'd find under the average slice of Kansas prairie. All of these conditions are considered to be important precursors to volcanic activity. The fires of 1988 dashed our illusions of this place being a stable, ever-familiar slice of landscape. One day, who knows when, volcanism may make that same point in a far more striking manner.

By the time darkness falls we are only a mile from the end of the trail, and though we're as weary as old elk after a hard winter, we reach the trailhead in splendid spirits, high on having shared what seemed like a considerable ordeal. We take off our packs and settle into a reclining position, when Jane comes up with the bright idea that I should moon Jim and Nancy as they return with the vehicles. Given my present state of elation, this sounds like a splendid idea.

After about twenty minutes, Jane identifies the lights coming up the road as those of our car, I turn and drop my nylon hiking shorts, bend over, and wait for the horn to honk and the laughter to begin. Unfortunately, the next thing I hear is a window being rolled down behind me, and a strange woman's voice saying, "Nice cleavage—but do I know you?" Sadly, it's not our Blazer at all, but one from Colorado with two women in it who were simply pulling over to ask if we knew of any camping spots nearby. Of course at this point my stature as a source of reliable information is somewhat compromised. After mumbling an apology I offer what I know as far as campgrounds, pray that they'll leave quickly, and then start looking around for the nearest badger hole to crawl in. Naturally, Jane finds all of this funny—you might even say hilarious—and to this day can pull herself out of a bad mood just by thinking about it.

•

We set off into the backcountry again on September 12, Jane's blisters healed, and not a drop of tequila running in my veins. The sky is clear, that flawless Prussian blue that hangs over the Rockies every autumn, and the steppes, thick and brown with Idaho fescue and bearded wheatgrass, are littered with the chalky bones of fallen bison and elk. As we ford Slough Creek I spot two trumpeter swans well upstream, floating in the current like tiny puffs of cloud. To me there's no more beautiful water bird in all of America than the trumpeter. The largest bird of its kind on the continent, it may often attain a wingspan of eight feet, doing so on a diet of twenty pounds of aquatic plants a day. Yet it remains the epitome of grace, what ballerinas might look like if they could fly. John James Audubon once assured his readers that upon spotting a flock of these graceful birds they would feel just as he did, "happier and freer of care than I can describe."

But trumpeters are also a reminder of how delicate the balance of life can be for some members of this ecosystem. Nesting only in the Yellowstone region and in Northern Canada and Alaska, in winter trumpeters have to concentrate on the small number of streams and lakes that never freeze, no matter how low the temperature. Even slight disturbance by skiers or snowmobilers may force them off these areas, which can place them in danger of starvation. By 1932 loss of habitat and hunting pressure reduced the population of trumpeters in the Yellowstone ecosystem to only sixty-nine birds; thanks in large part to superb efforts by the U.S. Fish and Wildlife Service at nearby Red Rock Lakes National Wildlife Refuge, today there are over five hundred.

We work our way west toward Hellroaring Creek, surrounded by a tumbling patchwork of open, grassy shoulders freckled with aspen and Douglas fir. The forests, in turn, shelter blankets of snowberry, sedge, pinegrass, Oregon grape, strawberry, and yarrow. Were you to walk through the vast fir stands to the south of here, by the end of the day you might find yourself begging for vertical relief. But from this more northern vantage point the park offers sizable helpings of form and profile—the ramparts of Mount Washburn to the south, the mighty Absarokas rising off to the east, and the high, grassy lip of the Buffalo Plateau towering above us to the north. From the lowest point in the park at mile-high Gardiner, Montana, to the highest peaks of the Absarokas is a spread of nearly six thousand feet. And in six thousand feet entire worlds can be formed—from warm, dry quilts of sage, to frigid sprawls of Arctic willow and woodrush.

In July, when the air is usually dry, the temperature drops nearly five degrees for every thousand feet of elevation gained. This means when it's ninety degrees outside of Gardiner, the summits of the Absarokas may be lucky to see sixty. Snow will typically start to build on the top of Mount Washburn by September 26; in Gardiner, just twenty miles away, accumulation won't begin until six weeks later, on November 8. Furthermore, Gardiner is typically free of the white stuff by April 18, while on the summit of Washburn, you can often still have a snowball fight until the third week in July.

Total annual precipitation in Yellowstone is also greatly influenced by the location of mountains. Areas in the western portion of the park receive significant amounts of precipitation, especially snow, as moisture-laden air drifts across the Snake River plains and is then pushed up by the high peaks, cooling as it rises. Since cool air can't hold as much moisture as warm air, storm clouds dump much of their cargo as soon as they reach this initial high line. This then reduces the amount of snow or rain these systems have to offer the interior of the park—a phenomenon known as rain shadow. In large part it's this cast of the high country that causes the southwest corner of the park to receive nearly seventy inches of precipitation annually (twice that of good Midwest farm country, though much of this is snow), while Gardiner receives ten to twelve inches, placing it just above a desert.

Yet much of Yellowstone's weather is also the result of various dances and wrestling matches between Pacific and Arctic air masses. Pacific air arrives here after first crossing either the Sierras, if it comes from the southwest, or the Coast, Cascade, and Bitterroot ranges, if it comes from the northwest.

Arctic air masses, on the other hand, usually come in cold and dry, dropping like stones across the wind-blown plains of Montana. Besides increasing precipitation by cooling off moist Pacific air masses, this Arctic air keeps the average monthly temperature near the center of Yellowstone a chilly 32.8 degrees. (Not that average means consistent. The record high in the park is 103, and the record low is −66— a rather sizable spread of 169 degrees.) In light of what is generally a chilly climate, the temperatures that Jane and I have experienced since we first started up the Stillwater— low to mid 80s nearly every day—seem like a gift from the gods.

In the end climate calls the tunes to which all other life forms must dance. There would be no great herds of bison or elk in the northern valleys and meadows of the central plateau if conditions had not favored the growth of grasses such as fescue and wheatgrass, and forbs like lupine, phlox, and groundsel. Grizzlies might not find the area so hospitable if the land was significantly drier, as there would be no yampa, biscuitroot, yarrow, and whitebark pine for them to feed on. But for the small, dry pocket of bluebunch wheatgrass, needle and thread, and junegrass growing on the lowlands at the north end of the park near Gardiner, no antelope would winter in the park at all. And, considering that fully half of all the moisture available to the region is found in whatever snow is lying on the ground on April 1, were there no spring storms heaving across the mountains, the plants, wildlife, and even the streams would be cut to a small fraction of what they are today.

As we descend toward the Yellowstone River, the landscape before us looks like something out of a western dream. Douglas fir and an occasional juniper pepper the hillsides, and there are long lazy drifts of fescue, wheatgrass, and sage. Vast deposits of till carried here by glaciers during the last ice age not only created this gentle maze of hummocks and twisted, hidden ravines but, more important, left nutrient-rich soils that could hold significant amounts of moisture. This ultimately helped turn the area into a paradise for grazing animals like elk and bison, the latter which we can see lying just below us—giant, shaggy lumps the color of chocolate cake, heads down in a wash of yellow grass.

By the time we reach the upper stretch of the Black Canyon of the Yellowstone, the heat has started to rise again, making the river far too inviting to resist. Although this far upstream the Yellowstone is generally too cool to linger in, today I lose count of the number of times I've jumped into the deep green eddies and then dragged myself out onto a slab of rock to warm like a lizard in the September sun. By midafternoon I know that the Black Canyon has already become one of my favorite places—not just for the scenery, which is splendid, but for the blend of river and rock and sun that leaves us feeling so pleasantly lost in the slow drift of the summer.

My affection for the Black Canyon wasn't shared by many early explorers, most of whom were forced to skirt around it on their way up the Yellowstone River. Lieutenant Gustavus C. Doane, a well-read, very capable soldier thought to have named this particular canyon, called it "grand, gloomy, and terrible; a solitude peopled with fantastic ideas, an empire of shadows and turmoil." While I may not agree with Doane's interpretation, I definitely think his choice of "Black Canyon" is more intriguing than "Third Canyon," which was the name used by early trappers and prospectors.

The trail continues to make a lazy meander to the northwest, hugging the river as it churns past dark cliffs and loosely knit huddles of pine. Past the lovely shimmer of Crevice Lake is Crevice Creek, which at this point ends its fast dance from the steep, rugged slopes of Ash Mountain. It was here, well inside the park boundary, that prospector John Knowles decided to build himself a cabin in the late 1890s. Not surprisingly, Knowles lost his humble abode almost as soon as government rangers stumbled across it. But by that time he'd made a gold strike worth close to forty thousand dollars, which proved more than enough for him to head for Chicago and rent the Old Iroquois Theater for a single night, open a full show to the public free of charge, and then invite the entire cast and audience to accompany him for a free drink in the nearest saloon. Knowles Falls, a beautiful fifteen-foot drop on the Yellowstone River just downstream from Crevice Creek, was named in honor of this generous man.

But John Knowles's wasn't the only story to rise along this stretch of river. A couple miles farther downstream is the location of the first cabin occupied by whites inside what would become Yellowstone Park, built in 1867 by a man named George Huston. During construction, as the story goes, Huston had some friends stop by, one of which made the rather blunt, unflattering comment that the place looked an awful lot like a turkey pen. Rarely has so casual a comment made such a lasting impression. While the cabin is long gone, the creek near where it stood still bears the name Turkey Pen. So does the high peak just to the south of the Yellowstone River, and, a littler further south still, a pass in the old roadway that miners traveled on their way to the gold fields at Cooke City.

From the point where the Yellowstone finally emerges into a dry, desertlike basin outside of Gardiner, Montana, it has roughly eight hundred more miles to go before losing itself in the brown waters of the Missouri. The Yellowstone has the distinction of being the last undammed major river left in the continental United States, having by some miracle already survived plans to plug it with reservoirs.

The river begins in a remote stretch of the Absaroka Mountains southeast of the park, on a wild, rugged face of Younts Peak, where very few people have ever trod. From there it flows through the yawning meadows of the Thoroughfare country, pours into the southeast arm of three-hundred-foot-deep Yellowstone Lake, and emerges twenty miles later from the northern shore, near Fishing Bridge. Next it makes an easy glide to the northwest past clumps of silver sage, hairgrass, and sedge, its quiet waters sprinkled with green-winged teals, mallards, and trumpeter swans. Rather abruptly, though, the still life is left behind as the river plunges twice over the ragged tiers of a collapsed volcano, first dropping

115 feet, and then 306 feet, finally roaring off into the Grand Canyon of the Yellowstone, the fluted walls coated in some of the most mystical colors imaginable. Once out of the canyon, the Yellowstone joins the Lamar, which is fresh out of its own beautiful valley to the east, and together they twist out of the park through the dark chasms of the Black Canyon.

Contrary to popular belief, the Yellowstone did not take its name from the bright yellows rocks lining the upper canyons. The appearance on a French map in the late 1700s of a "R. des Roches Jaunes" (river of yellow rocks) was a literal translation of words used by the Minnetaree Indians. But the Minnetaree lived on the Missouri River near present-day Mandan, North Dakota, and almost certainly would have had no knowledge of any portion of the river this far upstream. Thus the name that most of us think so perfect, especially after we gaze over that beautiful stretch of canary-colored rock beneath the lower falls, in all likelihood was a description of a rather subdued line of sandstone cliffs, hundreds of miles downstream.

To ardent fishermen the Yellowstone is clearly a branch of heaven's own waters. In 1877, no less than General William Tecumseh Sherman declared it "the best trout-fishing stream on earth." And while at first that may seem a bit presumptuous—the words of a man merely having a good day on the end of a fishing pole—through the years many others have agreed. In Montana over a hundred miles of the Yellowstone, from the park to the Boulder River near Big Timber, has been classified as a blue-ribbon trout stream.

Coming out of this leg of our trek right into the town of Gardiner has distinct advantages, as we can simply cross the Yellowstone, turn right on Park Street, and slip into a bar to down a few cold beers. The bartender is a laid-back fellow of thirty-five named Dan, and when he sees our packs he immediately wants to know all about our trip. Somewhere along the line, I think it's during the third round of drafts, the conversation turns to grizzlies. Now you should understand that there are few residents of this town without firsthand knowledge of wildlife. After all, in winter there are times when you can hardly walk out of the house for all the elk feeding and lounging in your yard. Elk routinely stare into the windows of the school, and last year the track team had to yield the practice field to a herd of bison. On the other hand, in dry falls, when the pickings are poor in the backcountry, it's hardly unheard of to walk down a dark alley and come upon either a black bear or grizzly picking through garbage cans.

"I wouldn't think a thing about grizzlies," Dan tells Jane, sensing her worry. "Other than one night out back of this bar, I've never had what you might call a close encounter, and I've been in the backcountry for close to twenty years." About that time a friend of the barkeep, a willowy young woman named Cindy, rushes in through the front door, needing to change the diaper on her four-month-old son. Dan tells her to have at it, which she does on one of the tables in the center of the bar, catching us up on all the latest gossip as she works.

Just as Cindy is pressing the tabs down on a new Pamper, another local comes in, sees our packs sitting in the corner, and steers the conversation back to grizzlies. But this fellow isn't so quick to reassure us of how benign they are. "Luke was over hunting north of West Yellowstone last year—you know Luke? Anyway, this griz spots him, and starts chasing his butt down an old fire road. Well, Luke makes for a climbing tree, but before he can get high enough, the bear manages to clamp his teeth on Luke's hunting boot. Didn't drag him out of the tree, but those damn teeth went right through the boot into his foot. Luke stays up there 'til the bear goes away, then climbs down and hobbles three miles back to his truck. Laughed my ass off when he told me. Those bears, though— they'll get ya if they're in the mood to."

The 750 residents of this town are an intriguing, even eclectic mix. While in summer a lot of the real characters get lost in a suffocating shuffle of tourists, on any given night you can amble down to the Blue Goose or the K Bar and kibitz with everyone from cowboys to fishing guides, biologists to miners. You can drink and dance, and you can fight and howl at the moon. You can win a bundle in a pool game, and then lose it all in a few hands of five card stud. Small though Gardiner may be, I always have a strong sense of never quite knowing what might come to pass here. Appropriately, the town takes its name from a wild, illiterate trapper named Johnson Gardner, for whom the nearby river was christened sometime in the early 1830s. Gardner is thought to have come west up the Missouri at the very dawn of the boisterous Rocky Mountain fur trade, and was at various times in the company of such famous mountain men as Jedediah Smith, Hugh Glass, and Jim Bridger.

While Gardner has often been written of as being as crude and cruel as any trapper to ever ply the Rockies (he once threw two Arikara Indian captives into a roaring bonfire), he was also incredibly brazen. His most famous caper, which took place well south of here, involved the theft of some seven hundred furs (a small fortune) from the Hudson Bay Company. Immediately afterward he managed to wrangle nearly two dozen of the Hudson men away from their boss, Peter Skene Ogden, by promising to pay them eight times what they were currently getting for their pelts. When Ogden tried to resist, Gardner is said to have drawn his gun, hauled up the American flag, and told the Hudson Bay chief in no un-certain terms to get off American soil. Never mind that the land actually belonged to Mexico. Given the tensions that existed between the United States and Great Britain at the time, it's something of a minor miracle that Gardner's brassy antic didn't result in a major conflict between the two coun-tries. Some historians have suggested that Gardner met his end at the hands of the Arikaras, who, paying him back for his earlier treatment of two of their warriors, scalped him and threw him into a bonfire.

The town of Gardiner is the end of this season's walking for me, a kind of exclamation mark for a journey that started a hundred miles ago, on the warm, rocky banks of the Still-water. From the sidewalk in front of the bar I can see the great stone arch that marks the northern entrance to Yellow-stone National Park. Most of the tourists have gone now, and the locals that pass by seem loose and happy, glad to be out and about again in a quiet town. On the other side of the street, Cindy lopes along holding her freshly changed baby close to her chest, calling and waving at nearly everyone she sees, raising her face and smiling into the warm September sun.

FOUR

It's nearly one in the morning on a cold February night. Four of us are speeding through the darkness down an empty highway, each staring sadly out the windows at icy fields of corn stubble, and dark, motionless lumps of Angus cattle. I'm sitting in the backseat behind the driver, and over his shoulder I watch as the needle on the speedometer creeps up to eighty, then ninety, then a hundred, and none of us cares much, because speed seems like an antidote to the gloom that's been rolling over us for much of the night—a kind of protest, like a driver in a funeral procession, angry and bitter at death, who suddenly wheels around the hearse and breaks free.

The source of our doldrums is a public meeting held in Billings for input on the Greater Yellowstone Vision Document, a Congressionally mandated effort by various land use agencies to draft a long-term management plan for the ecosystem. It was the largest turnout ever in this city for a Forest Service meeting, and the place was near flood stage with anti-government sentiment. Angry men wearing the yellow armbands of the prodevelopment movement sat in folding chairs with their arms crossed, casting hard, silent stares. With a few exceptions, those who stood to speak for conservation did so somewhat tentatively, as if they weren't completely sure that a mob wasn't waiting for them just outside the back door.

According to the majority, land managers (and their co-horts, the environmentalists) want nothing more than to turn this region into one big national park, where residents will lose the right to hunt, fish, ranch, mine, snowmobile, motor-cycle, or cut timber. Personally, I have no desire that this place ever be turned into a homogeneous land of the groovy, where the wealthy vie for the right to have the best view of the wilderness while everyone else ends up moving someplace where taxes and rent are still affordable. A strong town, like a strong forest, is one with diversity—miners, hippies, log-gers, hardware salesmen, ski bums, waiters, ranchers, musi-cians, builders, shopkeepers, and philosophers.

I know that most people do care about what happens to this place—care about it the way that ranchers did in the early 1970s, when they fought a federal proposal to lace the northern Great Plains with coal strip mines in order to achieve "national energy self-sufficiency." Care about it the way cit-izens across the state of Montana did when they struck down a plan to dam the Yellowstone, the nation's longest free-flow-ing river. Care about it the way that a logger from St. Regis, Idaho, did, who sat across from me in a coffee shop one May morning with his teeth clenched, angry that Champion had decided to clear-cut an entire river bottom where he and his son had been fishing together for fifteen years.

While it's hardly unusual to find conservationists and work-ers in extractive industries sitting on different sides of the stadium, right now companies are trying to escalate our scrimmages into all-out wars. People for the West!, an indus-try brute in grass-roots clothing, is spending countless hours riling up conservative residents in small towns with horror stories about the environmentalist agenda, and then gener-ously offering to help them do something about it—driving miners and loggers to public input meetings to protest plan-ning efforts, and generally arming them with fistfuls of ex-traordinary misinformation. For example, People for the West! has warned repeatedly about how the Vision Document is an attempt to expand the park, as if federal land acquisition was no longer decided by Congress, but by the superintendent of Yellowstone. Other claims say that hunting will no longer be allowed in the forests, that the document sets policies for Indian lands (a shameless exploitation of sympathies for Native Americans), that new roads and facilities for tourism won't be built—all of which are utterly untrue.

Such hype is no accident. It is carefully designed to upset reasonable planning efforts, to pit potential allies against one another (ranchers and conservationists concerned about a coal mine, for instance), so that extractive corporations can maintain a heavy hand over what happens to federal lands in the years ahead. "Industry is capitalizing on the fact that public lands are used by so many different groups," one Forest Service official told me. "It's clearly to their benefit to tear people apart." People for the West! is one of the wealthiest corporate-sponsored organizations in the United States, frequently receiving contributions ranging from ten thousand to a hundred thousand dollars from companies like Chevron, Nerco Minerals, and Hecla Mining. The group has nearly two dozen chapters in the state of Montana alone; for a time, executive operations were run from offices at Noranda's subsidiary, Crown Butte Mining, as well as from the headquarters of Basin Mines, near Helena.

Other such industry-sponsored groups are forming almost weekly with the purpose of furthering one or more of the causes that appeared on a 1988 manifesto known as the Wise Use Agenda. This agenda includes such stellar goals as pushing for mining and oil exploration in all national parks, wildlife refuges, and wilderness areas; the systematic logging and replanting of all ancient forests; the removal of all restrictions on wetlands development; and the elimination of protection under the Endangered Species Act for any creature considered "nonadaptive," or "lacking the vigor to spread in range." In fact, there are now more than 250 of these organizations; together they form what is often referred to as the "wise use" movement. My personal favorite, and a shoo-in for the most absurd choice of name, is Environmentalists for Jobs, organized in 1990 by the president of the Chicago Mining Corporation. (It was seven employees of the Chicago Mining

Corporation, incidentally, who in the fall of 1989 forced their way into a home in Pony, Montana, and proceeded to harass a group of people trying to review the impacts of a proposed gold mining operation; the next meeting had to be held with a deputy sheriff posted outside the door.)

The sad thing is that the harassment, both by politicians and by thugs, seems to be working. In October of 1990, Director Lorraine Mintzmeyer of the Rocky Mountain Region of the National Park Service says she met with the principal Deputy Assistant Secretary of Fish, Wildlife and Parks, Scott Sewell. Sewell informed her that certain politicians had exerted a great deal of pressure on the White House to gut the existing version of the Greater Yellowstone Vision document. Sewell went on, says Mintzmeyer, to tell her that then–White House Chief of Staff John Sununu had contacted him personally, informing him that the document was to be rewritten entirely, that it would retain the appearance of a professional and scientific effort by the agencies but that in reality it would be based on strictly political concerns. Mintzmeyer said later that though she believed the revised document didn't meet the level of professional analysis required by Congress, saying so "would not be received positively." As of March 1992, the Greater Yellowstone Coordinating Committee, which produced the Vision Document, was replaced with a "Unit Management Team" (the word Yellowstone was evidently too volatile). Regional representatives will no longer participate in the meetings—a fact that wouldn't have made much difference to Lorraine Mintzmeyer, as she was transferred to Philadelphia, and shortly afterward, retired.

It's worth noting that Mintzmeyer was considered by many to be one of the most loyal, devoted team players the Park Service ever had. (This stands to reason, since women who are mavericks are rarely permitted to rise to the upper ranks of male-dominated agencies.) Mintzmeyer was obviously uncomfortable standing before the annual meeting of the Greater Yellowstone Coalition in the spring of 1992, and blowing the whistle on the deal making that now threatens the integrity of our national parks. "The parks are being choked to death by the actions of special interests and their political patrons," she explained. "Political intervention has led to such a dilution of the NPS purpose that I fear for the service's very survival. No study or report can be assumed to be trustworthy because it is impossible to know whether the base-level data was tinkered with, in what way, and how much. I would advise you that any study after 1983, and definitely after 1988, must be suspected of being scientifically or professionally unreliable."

When I first came to Montana in 1987, it was a shock to find that a state with such a long, proud history of resisting big business was fast becoming little more than an errand boy to corporate power brokers. It wasn't all that long ago that residents here were fighting corporate trusts as if they were invented by the devil himself. "These people are my enemies," independent industrialist Fritz Heinze growled about Standard Oil to fifteen thousand cheering miners on the steps of the Butte Courthouse in 1903. "But they are your enemies too. If they crush me today, they will crush you tomorrow. They will force you to dwell in Standard Oil houses while you live—and they will bury you in Standard Oil coffins when you die." As recently as 1981, when *Washington Post* editor Joel Garreau declared in *The Nine Nations of North America* that this region of the country "faces a future in which it will be chewed up and spit out to light the lights from Los Angeles to Boston," more than a few Montanans were determined to prove him wrong.

The recent shift in attitude is less an indication of changes in the hearts of residents, than that resource-based corporations have become more masterful at hiding their big sticks under a cloak of "grass roots" activism. Plum Creek, for example, has been remarkably effective at using so-called "wise use" groups to blame timber-related job losses in Western Montana on environmentalists. Never mind the fact that in order to raise quick capital in the 1980s the company clearcut its properties at thoroughly unsustainable rates, and then dumped the land at fire-sale prices. "Both Plum Creek and Champion had abandoned sustained-yield forestry and were logging their lands as rapidly as possible," writes former Missoulian reporter Richard Manning in his fine book, *Last Stand*. "The practice was doubly damaging in that it would, in less than a decade, create a widespread shortage of logs that would undermine the long-term health of the corporation's own industry."

Never mind that since 1950, 33 percent of all timber-related jobs have been lost to automation, that for years millions of raw logs poured overseas, sometimes illegally, taking thousands of mill jobs with them. In the case of mining, the smallest fluctuation in metal prices or even changes in tax laws have eliminated more mineral-related jobs than the most fervent Earth First-er could manage in a lifetime of heated battle.

The way that Plum Creek cut trees in western Montana not only traded hundreds of future jobs for quick cash, but in many cases severely damaged the land's natural ability to heal and regenerate. Now they are pushing hard to increase cuts on the national forests, to turn the public woods into little more than vanilla-flavored lumber farms.

"It always comes down to profits," says a former reclamation biologist from southern Montana. "When the Reagan administration came in, companies were suddenly given lots more room to reclaim their mining operations as they saw fit, instead of according to the letter of the law." Up until 1980 this biologist had a good business growing native plant stock in greenhouses, which he then sold to corporations for reclamation. It folded less than a year after the election, when managers discovered they could get their bond monies released by, as he describes it, "tossing out a few bags of wheatgrass." What will such places look like in fifty years? Which will trickle down to the people in the face of such economic free flight, substantial income or merely the real cost of proper reclamation?

At Joliet we pull into the J Bar for a couple of beers and a game of pool. I stand beside a jukebox stuffed with country songs, waiting for my shot, gazing over to the bar at a long line of old men in scuffed boots and nappy cowboy hats. With every strum of Garth Brooks's guitar I find myself wishing more and more that I had been young in this place when they were young, when there really was enough land to soak up the abuses, when it was easy to wash away the taste of exploitation with the lingering illusion of a frontier.

It's easy to understand how, as far as some of these guys are concerned, the notion of managing the region by long-range planning not only seems unnecessary, but absurd. "If it isn't broke," one rancher told me, "then don't fix it." But I came here from a broken place. And in that place there was also a time when few could imagine that the nation would one day march across the length and breadth of it, turning all but a tiny fraction of its forests and prairies into factories and car lots and shopping malls. In fact, that's the biggest difference of all between those guys at the bar and me; they believe there are plenty of open unshackled places left for everyone, while I see them fading as fast as snow drifts in a March chinook. Without that sweet scent of the hinterland floating on the breeze, what will the old families of Montana really pass on to their kids, but a thin, pale ghost of the land most swear made them what they are—the land that gave them strength and solace and hope?

How do we cross the lines and labels of tree hugger and redneck? How do we find and hold the common ground? I confine myself to those who stand around the edges of this pool table, while those with yellow armbands are no doubt doing the same in some other bar not far away. As long as the corporate wedge is driven between us we'll hide in the folds of those who think most like we do, missing all that's useful in the visions of the other side.

FIVE

Winter lies too long in country towns," wrote Willa Cather, "hangs on until it is stale and shabby, old and sullen." She must have been talking about Montana. For here there really is no spring—just early winter, midwinter, and late winter. And despite the numbing cold of January and February, in the end it is late winter that will get you: April with its wild winds that sneak up in the middle of the night, sending garbage cans tumbling down the gray alleyways; and May, teasing you out into the open with just the shirt on your back, then sending you home against the teeth of a blizzard. This is truly a nonseason, the only changes being the size and color of the snow piles in the IGA parking lot, swelling and whitening with every new storm, then quickly sinking back again into dirty gray.

The shopkeepers of Red Lodge, happy to be shoveling sidewalks so long as the ski area was open, now use their shovels more like weapons, shoving and jabbing at the snow, resigning themselves to the fact that only good weather can bring the tourists back. High schoolers sit on the wall outside the bank in clothes much too light for the temperatures, looking bored and sullen, suspended, like Vladimir and Estragon waiting for Godot. In Native American myth this season is said to be the time when the five brothers of the North are

locked in a fierce wrestling match with the five brothers of
the South; no matter how hard we seem to cheer for the
Southern team, there are times when I wonder if they will
ever really win.

It is on the cusp of this nontime, when midwinter is drifting
to late winter, that I don my pack and skis and set out for a
solo crossing of the Gallatin Mountains, on the northwest
corner of the Yellowstone ecosystem. My starting point is Tom
Miner Basin, well above the drift of the Yellowstone River
through Paradise Valley, above herds of elk pawing at the
ground for mouthfuls of fescue and timothy, above Claire
Prophet and the faithful of the Church Universal and Triumphant, waiting patiently with their fuel storage tanks and
bomb shelters and food supplies—waiting like those high
school kids on the bank wall, though not so much for the
beginning of anything as for the end.

Volumes of bitter prose have been written since God first
told the Church Universal and Triumphant to set up camp in
the Paradise Valley. We've watched in anguish as bomb shelters and trailer towns went up, where before there was only
the easy drift of open country. I remember standing in a Livingston food co-op a couple of years ago, leafing through a
church-sponsored newspaper. In the back was an assortment
of rather unusual classified ads, one placed by a single mother
from the East looking to grubstake a young man with four
thousand dollars' worth of bomb shelter space, in return for
his providing basic labor and protection to her and her children. I found the image bizarre, even tragic. Here was one of
the wildest valleys left in America, and now thousands of
frightened people were hustling for concrete bunkers in the
hope of inheriting whatever might be left after the scorch and
poison of a nuclear war.

It's true that the church has made some major blunders
since its arrival, most notably the accidental discharge of
32,000 gallons of fuel into beautiful Mol Heron Creek. But by
and large I think conservationists have used it as scapegoats
for the anger we have at unregulated development in general.
It is a biting reminder of our lack of zoning laws, and to a

lesser extent, of the fact that the Forest Service was for a time locked in negotiations to buy this very same land from Malcom Forbes. No matter what you think of CUT, the truth is that these twelve thousand acres probably would have been worse off had a developer latched on to them and sliced them into twenty-acre ranchettes, as is happening throughout much of the rest of the ecosystem.

In just the Wyoming and Montana counties of the Greater Yellowstone region there are right now 1 million acres of platted and unplatted subdivisions of two hundred acres or less. The bulk of the neighborhoods that do actually evolve will be along river corridors, near riparian areas, and in critical winter range. (Fully 80 percent of the elk winter range in the Yellowstone Valley is on private land.) Without a strong push for zoning, rural subdivisions, even more so than mining and logging operations, will sound the death knell for large numbers of elk, grizzly, and antelope in the years to come.

The day Jane drops me off at the trailhead is sunny and warm, the sky so bright that it hurts to look at it. If it stays like this for long, the chance of snowslides will increase significantly. The avalanche reporting service assured me this morning that there was only moderate danger, but just to be safe I do a snow profile, which involves digging a small pit and then checking the basic structure of the snowpack for whatever weaknesses might exist between the various layers. An icy crust on the surface, for example, may produce a large volume of water, which in turn tends to dissolve the bonds between the ice sheet and the slab of snow underneath.

Even with moderate avalanche danger it would be better to have another person along. But those I've asked can't go. And besides, I'm secretly thrilled to be heading alone into a place where winter still lies ten feet thick and white, where tonight the full moon will rise over the Paradise Valley, bathing the sharp crags of the northern Absarokas in a wash of eerie blue light.

The lower portion of my route has been open to logging trucks, which have turned what would have been a modest layer of skiable snow into a muddy quagmire. I seal my boots once again, hoist my pack and shoulder the skis and poles, and squish up the road toward the mountains. After a mile or so I pick up two sets of ski tracks on the shoulder, about a day old, as well as a fresh set of prints from a pair of hunting boots. Clearly, my trip will be much easier if these skiers are headed for the same pass that I am, since then I won't need to break trail. The down side of it is that it will be much harder to talk myself into that silly "pathfinding through the wilderness" fantasy that I so much enjoy; pathfinding, that is, with a full set of topographic maps, and a major highway twenty-five miles to the west that I couldn't miss if I were snow-blind.

At the two-mile mark I reach the snow-choked roads of Tom Miner Campground, and there find the young man who's been leaving the boot prints. He's a rugged, cowboy-looking sort, about twenty, with black hair and an easy, Sunday-afternoon kind of smile. We talk for a while, and he tells me that he's a business major at Montana State University. He's here looking for elk antlers, which he'll then sell in Bozeman to help pay his college tuition.

"I'll get about ten dollars a pound for these," he explains, lifting one of two five-point racks he holds in his hands. "All told, these two are probably worth close to a hundred and fifty bucks."

About the time I've figured out how many antlers it would take to pay for a new printer for my computer, he confesses that today has been especially good hunting. "I've gone out lots of times and not found a thing. And then I'm out the gas money it took to get there."

"Still," I offer, "it must beat flipping burgers at McDonald's."

"No question. Beats doin' anything in town."

Antler hunting, though a time-consuming moneymaker at best, is actually fairly common in the national forests of the Rockies. While craftspeople turn antlers into everything from belt buckles to chandeliers, a large chunk of the market exists because of heavy demands for horns and antlers in the Far

East, where people use them in various medicines, tonics, and even aphrodisiacs. In Jackson Hole the Boy Scouts have been collecting antlers under special permit from the National Elk Refuge since the late 1950s, which they then sell at a May auction in the town square. Last year that auction brought in a very respectable $76,000. While the troop kept only $14,000 of that, donating the rest to buy pellet feed for refuge elk, it sure beats selling light bulbs or hawking car washes at the corner gas station.

Of course high prices on such items is an added incentive to poachers. Each year thirty or more tons of antlers are taken illegally from within Yellowstone Park itself—many from an area that lies just to the south of here. Some park officials have gone so far as to say that 90 percent of all antlers dropped by the animals of Yellowstone in a given year are removed illegally by horn hunters; one notorious hunter claims to have removed three to four thousand pounds of antlers from the park every year for the past fifteen years. In some cases antlers are also obtained by shooting the animals first, or even running them to exhaustion with snowmobiles. Several years ago eight elk were found scalped near Slough Creek Campground; when rangers came across them, one was still floundering in the snow.

The typical poacher takes his ten- to twenty-pound racks during the day (preferably not after a fresh snow, though, since then his tracks are easier to follow), caches them somewhere well out of sight, and removes them between three and six o'clock in the morning. If while out collecting antlers, a hard-core poacher has the chance to bring down a grizzly bear, worth three to four thousand dollars, or even a large mule deer, whose meat might bring in $150, so much the better. Coyotes and beaver are also taken for their fur, while trophy poachers tend to concentrate on bighorn rams, mule deer, and male moose. Even trumpeter swan eggs have been taken on occasion, as have fledgling peregrine falcons, which are then sold to unsuspecting falconers. Unfortunately, only about 2 or 3 percent of the poachers operating in and around Yellowstone Park are ever caught.

In some ways the notion of using antlers and horns in tonics, and to a limited extent, as aphrodisiacs, reminds me of the "like cures like," or "doctrine of signatures" philosophies that for a time drove the plant lore of both European and Native American cultures alike. The basic assumption was that most medicinal plants bore specific, obvious clues as to how they should be used. Thus Chinese lantern, with its bladder-shaped sepals, was used to treat infections of the urinary tract. Got heart or liver trouble? Look for plants with heart-shaped or liver-shaped leaves. Need to increase breast milk in a nursing mother? Just look for a plant with milky juice. In Europe one of the more intriguing applications of such thinking was to use fern spore, which is essentially invisible to the naked eye, to render humans invisible as well. "We have the receipt of fern seed," Gadshill tells Chamberlain in Shakespeare's *Henry IV*. "We walk invisible." Hunters sometimes collected fern spore, usually around Midsummer's Eve, and then carried it in pouches on their belts to escape detection by game. I wonder: Did spies try to sneak into foreign castles and steal the plots of wars? Did suspicious husbands use it to catch their wives in the arms of other men?

Given the widespread acceptance of various "like cures like" theories, it's no surprise that some cultures would decide to use antlers, which to a large degree are simply tools for establishing male breeding rights, as either an aphrodisiac or as an ingredient in tonics designed to increase vitality. Still, while I'd hardly want to bankrupt the Jackson Boy Scouts, I'm convinced that the world's wildlife would be far better off if horns and antlers were no more than intriguing curiosities. Maybe psychologists could work with us to build an entirely new collection of symbols for male vitality and sexual prowess—say, a vegetable symbology, filled with zucchinis and cucumbers and bananas.

The college student is the last person I will see in three days. Almost from the time we say our good-byes and I begin my climb through the forest, the world becomes amazingly quiet, hushed in a way that only winter can manage. When I stop to rest, the slight rustle of my pack and the sound of blood pushing past my temples are the only clues to the fact that I can still hear at all. As the day warms, the silence is broken occasionally, first by lumps of wet snow sliding off the branches of the subalpine fir, and later, by the squawk of Clark's nutcrackers, sounding even more boisterous than usual against the general calm of the day.

Over the years I've come to appreciate the raucous nut-cracker, if not for his singing, then certainly for his reputation as an itinerant wanderer. Rather than being satisfied with a modest patch of predictable forest, this bird ranges all over the place, patrolling certain sweeps of alpine tundra for the chance to swipe a ptarmigan egg, making regular rounds of campgrounds in hopes of finding a stray piece of sandwich dropped during a recent picnic, and in winter, hopscotching up and down mountain ranges from one remote timbered valley to another. Appropriately, these birds have a special penchant for pine nuts, and can often be seen hammering the daylights out of a cone in order to get to the goodies inside. (It seems likely that when Lewis and Clark first discovered this bird in 1805 it was doing just that, a habit that caused them to refer to it as "a new species of woodpecker.") Nut-crackers even have a special cheek pouch beneath the tongue where they can stuff several nuts for easy transport. On oc-casion thousands of the birds may suddenly push well beyond their normal range, often showing up on the fringes of the West Coast. More than likely such movements are the result of poor nut crops on the inland range, though personally, I prefer to think of it as an advanced form of group tourism.

A pair of wings, I think, would be nice right now. It's hard to imagine a time when physical condition (or lack thereof) becomes more noticeable than when mushing up a mountain through the snow with sixty pounds on your back. Given this fact, the packed ski tracks I'm following westward above Trail Creek seem more and more like a gift. I'm so happy about them, in fact, that when they turn right up a side canyon on a high line above Dry Creek, I manage to convince myself that the previous skiers did this simply so that they could cross the ravine upstream, where it's much shallower. This detour,

I tell myself, would spare a person the need to make a hundred-foot drop to the bottom of the side canyon, and then have to climb up nearly two hundred feet to get out on the other side.

But after a mile or so it becomes clear that these tracks aren't just maintaining altitude, as they would be if they were going to round the head of the canyon, but are climbing steadily. More than likely the people who left them were telemark skiers bound for the high, open terrain on the southeastern flanks of Ramshorn Peak. Once I realize this, I'm faced with having to make a decision. I can retrace my steps back to the canyon mouth, or else make a steep drop through the timber, cross the creek, and, holding my elevation, begin working my way back out toward Trail Creek.

Never one to choose backtracking as my first option, I begin dropping through the timber. Telemarking under the weight of a full pack isn't without its problems, and before long my knees are turning to Jell-O I find myself wanting to ease up out of the turns a bit, but the tight growth of the trees, denser the further down the slope I go, keeps me locked into honest sweeps. My brother delights in reminding me that as a kid I had something of a reputation for sledding headfirst into trees; I can still remember lying awake on the couch in the living room after some family outing while my mother watched for signs of concussion. Up this remote canyon in the Gallatin Range, now off even the slightest hint of trail, is clearly no place to try knocking down timber with my head.

The last hundred yards before reaching the creekbed is like skiing through a booby trap. The downed timber looks like a scatter of giant pickup sticks just tossed from the can, too high to ski over and impossible to go around. I can step over the small logs, but I have to lean on the big ones with my hip and then slide the skis over, trying to keep the backpack from getting snagged on the stubs of old branches in the process. When I finally do reach the creek I find it crisscrossed with beautiful but fragile snow bridges, many of which I have no choice but to cross. A couple of times when I step on one it slumps a foot or so, leaving me to scale the other side by kicking my skis into whatever vertical bank remains; fortunately, none of the bridges collapses altogether and sends me plunging into the water below. Though from a practical standpoint this drainage is trying, from an aesthetic point of view it's pure magic. The clear, gentle waters of Dry Creek are running through a fantasyscape of cornices and finely sculpted ice. Huddles of buff-colored rock pillars line much of the creek, most wearing derbies or top hats fashioned from the purest, whitest mounds of snow. The mature trees are thick, but in a full wash of sunlight they lend a stately rather than a somber look to the canyon. As I'm busy admiring all this, I hear a sudden, loud crash somewhere downstream. It's probably the moose who's been leaving a line of fresh tracks along the west bank of the creek; though I quicken my pace, I never do manage to catch up.

By the time I reach the hills above Trail Creek again, the mud, the downed timber, the snow bridges, and far too much time over the past several months spent parked in front of the word processor, have left me more than ready to make camp. Though I have a tent, I've always wanted to spend a winter night like John Muir did, snuggled in the deep cavities that lie beneath the branches of old conifers. I find a fir that fits the bill perfectly, and what's more, offers an incredible view of Tom Miner Basin and Paradise Valley to the east and the immense, heroic-looking peaks of the Absarokas beyond. I build a small fire at the edge of my tree cave, have a bite to eat and a cup of tea, and settle back to wait for the rising of the moon.

In many Native American cultures, the sight of the moon and sun arcing across the sky are reminders of a story about a brother and sister of long ago, who, no matter how hard they tried, just couldn't get along. Unable to stand it any longer, one day the sister grabbed a burning stick from the lodge fire, and rose up quickly through the smoke hole of the tipi. "You won't escape me that way!" cried her brother, and he grabbed an even bigger burning log from the campfire, and drifted out the smoke hole after her. And so both keep running across the sky country, the sister bringing moonlight to our nights, the brother, sunlight to our days.

At first I fear I'll fall asleep and miss the sister running through the night, but it turns out there's little chance of that. Of all the times to self-destruct, my wonderful, guaranteed-for-life Thermarest mattress has chosen this night to spring a leak, leaving me plastered against a cold blanket of snow. As the evening wears on I end up stuffing thermal blankets, a down jacket, a felt jacket, spare clothes, and whatever else I can lay my hands on underneath me, but at best I end up with only a small area of my shoulders or hips safe from the grating cold. Finally I prop my head and shoulders on the pack, stuff whatever insulating material I can find under the small of my back, and pull my knees into the air so that only the bottom of my feet are touching the ground. I look and feel like a bent spoon. Whatever cold does manage to seep in when I dare to stretch out—especially if I fall asleep in that position—doesn't stop at the skin, but goes straight to the bone, aging my body on the spot, leaving me feeling like an old Eskimo who's making his last drift out to sea on the back of an ice floe. As you might imagine, this night leaves me with a profound appreciation for man's mastery over fire.

The moon makes an easy drift through the cold black of the sky, casting the entire landscape in soft whispers of light. At one point in the middle of the night the scene becomes so enchanting that I climb out of my sleeping bag and take a long walk atop the frozen snow, first to peer into the dark, timbered shadows along Trail Creek, and then at the bright, nearly surreal glimmer of the mountain peaks to the south and east. This surely must be what Tennyson meant when he wrote of the "long glories of the winter moon."

Sheep Mountain, rising nearly 4,500 feet above the snowy flats of Tom Miner Basin, completely dominates the scene. My imagination drifts upward into the patchwork of steep meadows and dusky stands of subalpine fir. For a moment I forget that I'm standing here shivering, and instead find myself searching for a suitable ski approach to the 10,095-foot summit. What an incredible view that small, flat piece of high country would afford, stretching across a hundred miles of the northland, from the windblown prairies of central Montana to the fire-blackened ghost forests of Yellowstone's Central Plateau. Still weighing the effort needed for such a trek, I make my way back to camp, resume my spoon position, and drift off to sleep.

The next morning dawns clear and bright, the light as clean as if sister moon had taken time out from her trip across the night sky to scrub the heavens free of all dust and debris. I'm anxious to work the cold out of my joints, so I wolf down a couple of packages of oatmeal and some dried fruit, restuff my pack, and head west again just as the sun clears the jagged crest of the Absarokas. During the night the snow has refrozen into a hard sheet, so I lay the wax on as thick as possible. Less than a mile from camp, though, much of it has already worn off, so I strap my skins on instead. (Skins, by the way, are long ribbons of fabric, plastic, or fur that lie against the bottoms of the skis. The outer surface has a bristly nap that catches the snow when the ski moves backward, to give you traction going uphill, but then lies flat when the ski moves forward, thus allowing a small measure of glide.)

In another mile or so I come to a place where the sides of the canyon steepen sharply, nothing below me but a long, hundred-yard slide on icy crust into the jumble of rocks and scattered timber that frame the banks of Trail Creek. In order to gain any purchase on the slope I have to kick the skis into the side hill as hard as I can with each step, always poised should they suddenly slip out from under me. About two-thirds of the way across the skis do kick out; fortunately I'm ready, and manage to punch my ice axe into the crust of the snow, stopping the slide before it picks up any real speed. Although this stretch is only a couple of hundred yards long, by the time I reach the other side my knees, ankles, and shins are worn out. A quick check of the map holds good news, though, in that the severity of the slope should start to ease considerably in another half-mile. Two miles beyond that the route will run nearly flat through a small park, climb with a sharp twist through a blind, S-shaped canyon, and finally top out on 8,500-foot Buffalo Horn Pass. It all looks very manageable, especially if the canyon up ahead has enough timber on it to keep the danger of snowslides to a minimum.

Sitting here dug into the snow on the side of this ravine, I'm amazed at how quickly things are warming up. Old globs of snow still resting on the fir branches from a previous storm are starting to drop like a carpet bombing, one muffled thud after another, and the crust that so nearly sent me sliding into the bottom of this gorge is already beginning to soften. To some extent, of course, this is a relief. But things are warming so fast that I know in another hour I'll have another problem on my hands: The snow pack is going to be the consistency of porridge—wet and heavy, and not likely to support 235 pounds of weight.

By eleven o'clock I'm still a half-mile from the end of the ravine, and the mercury of my pack thermometer has climbed beyond the fifty-five-degree mark. Conditions have gotten so bad that along one stretch I'm not only sinking above the knee, but after each step a thick ooze of white, icy sludge caves in on top of my skis, requiring me to literally dig them free by hand before I can lift them out again. For a long while I fight the situation, trying to muscle them out of the slop until my thighs are shaking with fatigue. Along one particularly bad stretch it takes close to thirty minutes to travel a hundred yards; at this rate I could ski from sunup to sundown and by tomorrow night still be a long way from the finish line.

When I finally do slog out of the ravine, conditions improve dramatically. In the forest, where the ground has been protected from the warm fingers of the sun, the snow is powdery and easy to kick through; along the upper flanks of Buffalo Horn Pass, it is still firmly compacted. In fact, things improve so significantly that at the top of the pass I decide to peel off my pack and explore the ridge for a while, gaining fabulously wild views to the west.

Unlike my ascent, which for the most part was along an

obvious, well-defined drainage, the trip down is across a wide, even flank of mountain wrapped in heavy timber. To pick up Buffalo Horn Creek without spending any extra miles, or worse yet, dropping into a ravine that might be thick with the same sludge that filled Trail Creek, means pegging a compass course and then skiing it as closely as possible. Since the trees are much too thick to pick out any landmarks, I have to stop every eighty or ninety yards to reestablish my compass line. Ah, but after doing this a couple of times it's obvious that the skiing is way too much fun for such interruptions. And so the compass goes back into my pocket.

I am floating in slow motion through deep white powder, past startled red squirrels who dash up the tops of fallen snags, past the play of sun and shadow in the spires of the conifers. There is no sound but for the slight hiss of ice crystals licking the bottom of my skis and the easy rustle of my jacket as I drop for another turn. An hour ago I was practically beached, grunting around, scooping slush off my skis, generally brooding about what further predicaments might lie ahead. Then suddenly it's as if none of that ever happened. Now I'm freefalling down the mountainside, curling through the snow and timber like I was fingerpainting with my feet.

This joyride goes on for nearly fifteen hundred vertical feet, after which I begin crossing a series of long, narrow glades, each one smooth and beaming in the April sun. There is no shortage of elk sign here: clusters of old tracks from animals that paused at the edge of the forest, too cautious to leave the protection of the timber, and also a line of fresh, very large prints from a lone elk who ventured out into the meadow not long before my arrival. I wonder if this was an old bull— thirteen, fourteen, sixteen years old—too aged to hold his breeding position against younger, stronger males. I can imagine this fellow in his prime at the vanguard of his herd, wallowing in sedge meadows each fall to cool the fever of the rut, sparring with his peers, bugling with abandon under the cold September moon. Most of his progeny, and there would have been many, were born one at a time in late May or early June, just shy of eight and a half months after the fall rut.

Sometimes his young could have been found trailing their mothers up from winter range just days after their birth, on the edge or even ahead of the retreating snow, abandoning an abundance of food in the valleys for the security of the hills. This bull would have been heading up too, but more than likely in the company of six or seven other males, all bound for some favorite summer spread of bluegrass and brome.

If indeed this old man has passed his prime, he'll likely not head up into the high country this summer with any other elk, but instead drift solo through the dark timber; perhaps on certain evenings he'll be found standing like a lone sentinel on some high, wind-scoured slope. It's even possible that this is the last of his winters. Next December might find him in the middle of some raging storm, wobbling across open range until he can go no further. At some point he'll founder in a drift, drop to his knees, and then roll onto his side. Then, with a sigh that no one on earth will hear, he'll push out his last breath, a last rush of warmth against the line of snowflakes settling on the broad, dark flare of his nose.

I stop building stories against the tracks in the snow at the point where the meadow begins to crease into a timbered ravine, bringing my carefree glide to an abrupt halt. The sides of the gulch have melted enough to reveal large rocks and fallen trees, while the streambed itself is a complicated maze of toppled snags and snow bridges that clearly cannot hold my weight without sloughing. I try several approaches. Sometimes I head up the bank, taking parallel steps over the downed timber. Then when the streambed clears I head back down and do the best I can with the snow bridges, literally jumping from the bank, trying to land the front half of my skis firmly on the other side to avoid falling in the stream should the bridge collapse altogether.

The thermometer hovers near sixty degrees. From a travel perspective, it would have been much easier for me to handle the cold and lingering darkness of February than to slog through this perplexing nonseason when winter begins to thicken and dissolve into spring. Not that I don't enjoy being able to ski in my shirt sleeves, or watching the streams start to bulge under the weight of the April sun. But I'm too bogged down to really enjoy it—my boots as saturated as the slabs of mud starting to show beneath the faces of the boulders and my back aching from hours of doing the hula over greasy logs and through collapsing banks of snow.

It hardly helps my disposition when during a food break I bring out the topos, only to find that tomorrow I'll have to traverse an extremely narrow canyon flanked by nearly vertical walls. If the warm temperatures continue, it seems almost certain that I'll end up working down a three-foot-deep ribbon of snow riddled with sink holes and collapsing trestles; when I'm not fighting for balance on the ledges, I may well be standing up to my ankles in icy creek water. With that, I toss back a few M & M's for courage and plod off again. Near dark I lay out my bedroll under an old fir with bare ground under it, consume my freeze-dried dinner as if I were stoking the boiler of a locomotive, and lie down to sleep the sleep of the bedraggled and the bushed, the pinched, the pooped, the weary, and the worn out. A cow moose clomps by sometime in the middle of the night. We exchange stares, but I am much too tired to engage in conversation. She stands there for a while as if she expects something from me, some kind of reaction, but my eyes slide shut, and when I open them again she is gone.

I'm up before sunrise. It seems safe to assume that if the ten remaining miles are anything like the last few, I'll be lucky to be out to the highway by dark, though Jane expects to meet me at three o'clock. The first two miles take nearly four hours. It stayed fairly warm last night, so the snow hasn't really firmed up, leaving me in slog mode almost from the very start. At one point, on a steep slope well above the sagging creek bottom, I find a long patch of cleared ground and decide to shoulder my skis and hike it. It is as slippery as gumbo, and I don't make a hundred yards before my right side is covered with mud, my ankles and heels sore from trying to arrest my slides.

In a bright, yawning stretch of meadow roughly a mile above the deep canyon I so dread, I come across two sets of snowmobile tracks. Bless the souls of these little snow-humpers; they've packed the snow so hard that I can fly down the meadow crouched like a racer, the sun sizzling on my face, ski tips slapping the ice, the land a beautiful blur of green and gray and white. Soon I reach the mouth of the canyon, and still the tracks hold firm. Where I thought I would be floundering I am schussing, coasting over dips and doodles, through willow thickets and past sheer walls of rock towering 1,200 feet above me. If yesterday was travail, this is no-holds-barred nirvana. After punching through the upper ravines this morning at the pathetic rate of a half-mile per hour, I cover the last six miles in under an hour.

It is two o'clock when I reach the highway. While waiting for Jane I sit by the side of the road and watch the Gallatin River roiling and flashing, gaining strength in the simmer of the sun. At the end of any wilderness trip there is always a sense of exhilaration, but never more so than when you've come face to face with physical exhaustion. It's in this elated posttrek state that my mind begins a kind of editing, a myth-making, really—grinding down the sharp edges of the hard times and buffing the good ones to make them shine. It's largely thanks to this blatant rewriting of the script that by the time Jane arrives, I've already promised myself that come next winter, I will head into the mountains once again.

SIX

I'm back on the trail in early July, but spring is only just starting to gather steam along the upper reaches of the high country. Yellow-bellied marmots are hustling down grassy runways to their favorite feeding areas, already fattening for the long winter ahead. White-crowned sparrows unleash their melodic trills well past the setting sun, while water pipets can be found searching for insects along the edges of the snow-fields. Coyotes, and even mountain lions, have returned to the tops of the mountains again, eager to hunt the greening sprawls of the tundra.

This southward trek between the Gallatin and Madison ranges is my first serious hike of the season, and by a mile out I'm regretting not having gotten into better condition. The truth is that I still think of mountain hiking in frames that I built in my early twenties. But that was fifteen years ago, and while my enthusiasm hasn't waned, my ability to dash up trails under full pack with impunity certainly has. The fact that I have a serious head cold and my traveling companion in the lead, Eric, has a bad case of gas, doesn't make things any easier. He christens me Captain Snotbox, I dub him Admiral Blowhole, and we trudge off through the foothills together like two kids in the throes of puberty, honking, tooting, laughing, and gasping for breath. Like clockwork, just when I'm starting to really falter, we stumble across an enormous bull moose, pushing hoofprints as big as my hand into the soft dirt. And once again, just seeing him leaves me feeling better.

The path makes a steady climb through alternating patches of spruce-fir forest wrapped in dim, murky light, as well as past brightly lit meadows stitched with geraniums, bluebells, paintbrush, forget-me-nots, and marsh marigolds. The paintbrush blooms are especially striking this year—ragged, raspberry-colored bracts tinged with a deep wash of scarlet. At the edge of one meadow is a large spruce tree; a good nine feet up the trunk are slash marks from some very large claws, as well as small tufts of bear fur. Bears have certain trees they rub against with delicious abandon, often standing on their hind legs and grabbing the trunk the way a cat leans up a scratching post. Some outdoorsmen believe that the height of the claw marks is a sign to potential rivals of the bear's size and stature (kind of like the four-foot-high line painted on the wall next to some of the crazier carnival rides; if you aren't at least this tall, move along).

There are also several large stumps lining the path, cut not by chainsaw but by axe. Maybe the trees were firewood for some rancher back in the 1940s, a burnt, tawny fellow who sat with the kids on bitter nights around his burning spruce logs, telling them of the days of gold and wolves, of buckboards rumbling up the Gallatin.

After nearly eight miles and 2,300 feet of climbing, we reach the long, narrow summit of Pika Point, named for that splendid little farming rodent who cuts grasses and turns them into hay by drying them on flat rocks. The place is thoroughly carpeted in buttercups, glacier lilies, and shooting stars, and offers nearly 360 degrees of astonishing view, the world tumbling from our feet in a riot of mountainscapes. Standing first on the western edge of the summit, we stare into the magnificent ramparts of the Madison Range. There is Lone Mountain and the mighty Sphinx, the latter home to a beautiful herd of snow-white goats. Imp Peak is flanked to the south by the rounded shoulders of Echo and Dutchman peaks, and then by the fat granite fingers of Hilgarde—a fortress that completely overwhelms the snow- and ice-bound basins lying directly below it, and a stern guard against easy access to the high country lakes that lie beyond. Immediately beneath these peaks is a tight weave of emerald green meadows, a paradise of good eating for local wildlife. To the south the land drops more gently into the green folds of Carrott Basin, and beyond that, rises and falls in a series of high ridges toward the northwest corner of Yellowstone. To the east are yet more meadows to savor—long green twists of grasses and forbs, backed by tattered waves of high country in the Lee Metcalf Wilderness.

For much of the summer it would be hard to stay on Pika Point because of a lack of water. But this week there are still patches of snow scattered about which can be easily melted for drinking and cooking. Even though it's early in the day, having clearly found paradise we decide it would be foolish to go any farther, so we toss off our packs and set out on a long walk to explore the southern lip of the ridge. Upon returning we break out a happy-hour feast of crackers and cheese and powdered lemon-lime drink mixed with generous splashes of rum. True, there are times when roaming the high country with a heavy pack on your back can be a grueling experience. But sitting in a lofty garden like this one, no one around for miles, and little to do but sip drinks and sigh over the scenery, is to scour all traces of drivel from your brain. Savoring the last rations of rum as the sun settles toward Sphinx Mountain, we move into the main eating event, which tonight centers around beef Stroganoff with fresh mushrooms. By the time dishes are done and the food is hung, the first elk are beginning to drift out of the forest into the lush meadows lying to the east. For now these animals have a catholic taste for forbs, dining on almost anything green they happen to find, be it geranium, lupine, or aster. Only later, when the forbs begin to cure and their nutrient content drops off drastically, will the animals switch to a diet made up predominantly of grasses.

•

About four o'clock in the morning I feel someone playing with my hair. Just as I'm about to nudge Eric awake and give him the news that I'm not the woman he thinks I am, I turn to see a mouse standing on his hind feet at the head of my sleeping bag. That his great ball of nesting material has risen and is now talking to him seems to leave him more incredulous than alarmed; in fact, it takes a fair amount of coaxing before he finally turns and ambles out of the tent, perhaps in search of a hiker that sleeps more soundly than I do.

By now I'm thoroughly awake, and struck with the urge to crawl out of the tent and take care of some pressing business. Looking up through the cool night air I find a sky so shot full of stars that I very nearly fall over backward looking at it. There is Perseus, Cassiopeia, Saggita, and Pegasus—all held against the "star trail," which is yet another name for what we know as the Milky Way. I spot a meteorite, and a minute later, two more. In this culture we often call these shooting stars; to many Native Americans, however, they are known as feeding or grazing stars.

Many cultures around the world believe that when a person dies, he or she rises into the heavens to become a star. Thus if a wife loses a husband or a woman a child, she will watch the sky night after night for the appearance of a new star; to find it holds nothing less than a sense of reconnection to the loved one who's passed on. Standing here atop this lonely ridge, I'm fascinated to think how it might feel right now to see the night sky as bursting with the spirits of my relatives and ancestors, all of them looking down on me with great affinity.

The Pleiades seem to be winking especially bright tonight above the eastern horizon, a tight cluster of stars known to the Blackfeet as the six brothers. As the story is still told today, in a Blackfoot camp of long ago there was a very poor couple who had six sons. Unlike most families, the boys' father could not hunt well, and so never acquired the precious red robes that other parents fashioned for their children from the hide of the young spring buffalo. Seeing the boys dressed in their old brown robes day after day, many of the people in camp teased them constantly. One morning the oldest boy called his five brothers together for a conference in the middle of a lonely prairie. "If we do not get the red robes next spring," he said, "then we shall leave this place and go into the sky."

Spring came and went, and still there were no red robes. So the brothers gathered up their dogs, and the oldest began to prepare a powerful magic that included placing weasel hair on the back of each boy. He then instructed everyone to close their eyes, and when he blew a small bunch of the hair out of his open palm, the boys began to rise into the house of the sun and the moon. The sun listened half-heartedly to the boys' dilemma, but in the end merely shrugged and asked what they expected him to do about it. The fourth brother spoke up right away, encouraging the sun to take the water from the people as a punishment for them having been so mean. But the sun wasn't convinced. The moon, on the other hand, so pitied the poor children that she promised to help them, but only if each would agree to stay in the sky forever. The moon repeatedly asked the sun for his help, but only on the seventh time did he finally agree.

The next day on earth was very hot—so hot, in fact, that the streams and lakes boiled, and then evaporated. The next night was warm and full of moonlight, and the people decided to take two dogs down to the riverbed and look for water. After a time the dogs began digging in the bank, and out of one of the holes emerged a cool spring. In the days that followed as each spring dried up, the dogs would dig another. This was how all the earth's springs were made, and today people still hold dogs in esteem for being the creatures to have uncovered them. As it happened, the old, white lead dog was a medicine dog, and on the seventh day he looked up into the sky and began to howl. Those howls were really prayers to the sun and the moon, explaining why the boys had no red robes, and asking them to take pity on the dogs below. (This, by the way, is why dogs howl at the moon.) Finally, on the eighth day, the rain came and the earth was replenished. And thus the bunched stars that we sometimes call the Pleiades are the six brothers, still huddled together in the house of the sun and the moon.

By five o'clock the stars begin to fade into a pale, flawless blue, that seamless drift from clear night into clear morning so typical of those short, sweet months of summer. After paying our respects to the dawn, catching the first rays of sun as they break over the rugged crest of the Gallatins, we grab a quick bite to eat, pack up the camp, and by eight o'clock are southbound for Carrott Basin. This area is so little used, and the south tier of the ridge so tightly woven with wildflowers, that the trail soon peters out altogether. We wander at will, falling across a web of gentle wrinkles in the land, most still capped at the heads by thick blankets of snow. Dozens of Clark's nutcrackers flit to and fro, feeding on scattered patches of white pine; when they're not whirling, diving, or eating, they sit in the tops of the trees like hawkers at a fair, squawking at other birds flying by.

Near the bottom of the basin, we stumble into a tremendous patch of wild onion, their nodding white blossoms freshly tinged with pink. While for many people onions tend to have about as much intrigue as potatoes and turnips, in fact they have been used—even revered—for thousands of years. The Egyptians believed that the universe existed in layers, the earth wrapped in the various strata of the heavens, and the onion became a sacred image of that universe. So serious was this particular symbology that oaths were administered not using a religious text as we do today, but with onions. And here was an icon with the added advantage of being good to eat! The Greek historian Herodotus claimed that onions were such an important foodstuff to the Egyptians that nine tons of gold were spent purchasing them for crews working on the pyramids.

By the Middle Ages both onions and garlic were being used to ward off evil spirits, some of which were thought to carry diseases like the plague. Folk healers concluded that the strong smell and flavor of onion and garlic, caused by high levels of sulfur compounds, meant that they could be applied to the skin as an antiseptic. (A great many herbalists continue to claim that onion helps fight acne, though it seems unlikely that any teenager would be willing to rub his face with one before heading out on a big date.) Modern studies have suggested that both onion and garlic not only help lower both blood pressure and cholesterol, but also act as antiinflammatory agents.

Just as another member of the lily family, the camas, often drove the seasonal movements of thousands of Native Americans, so too was the wild onion an important factor in deciding the location of summer camps. What's more, the explorers Lewis and Clark, various trappers, and a hungry, hell-bent General George Crook, pushing his men hard in pursuit of the Sioux after the Battle of Little Bighorn, all were extremely grateful to find patches of onion growing along the way.

Given the profusion of onion and the general lack of visitors to this basin, Eric and I whip out our spoons and set about digging a few of the precious bulbs for dinner. A few hours later, on the fringe of a gentle meadow sloping into the chiseled faces of the Madison Range, we find a land stitched through as far as the eye can see with the pink, bell-shaped blossoms of western spring beauties. Spring beauties are also edible, the roots tasting radishlike when raw and close to a potato when boiled, and their pungent leaves make as good of a salad green as anything you'll find in the kitchen of Spago's. I collect a couple of handfuls of the leaves, and tonight we have a full complement of hors d'oeuvres—the piquant, earthy taste of onions by the stalk, and spring beauty leaves served with hot pepper and a splash of lemon juice.

Earlier today the sky let loose with one of those classic midafternoon thunderstorms, and now the air is clean and cool and full of the smell of conifers. The meadows, already washed in a deep kelly green before the storm began, appear even richer now; from an elevated bench overlooking the far reaches of Carrott Basin, the land looks like Ireland on Rapid Grow. After dinner we head up to this bench, binoculars in hand, anticipating the time when elk will start to move out from the shadows of the conifers to fatten on the lush fields of forbs. Sure enough, about an hour before sunset the first movements begin—first one cow, then several, then a small string of striking five- and six-point bulls, each remarkably regal and august, lords who have come to survey the queen's pastures. When twenty animals have drifted into the lowlands to the west, we move down the ridge and check the action to the north. There we see two young bulls dash out of the woods, chasing each other through the meadows like spring ponies, leaping in great, exaggerated arcs, zigging and zagging, and then stopping to toss their heads, as a person might do after downing a big gulp of strong whiskey.

And still the play unfolds. A bull moose drifts out just west of the dancing elk. In the balcony seats high on the shoulders of Sage Peak are five bighorn sheep lying in a loose cluster, resting, taking occasional nips at the bunches of grass lying at their feet. Two of the animals appear to have rather large sets of horns, but none wears the rack of the truly old ram. In the eldest animals horns often become so large that they start to impede the animal's vision, leading the rams to grind the tips off by rubbing them against the rocks.

Sheepeater Indians made powerful composite bows out of the thick ridges that line the tops of these horns. The two horns were removed from the skull, heated, and straightened, and then each one was trimmed into a tapered wand roughly two feet long. The ends of the two pieces were then beveled, and a small piece of horn was placed over the joint. Finally the joint was wrapped in wet rawhide, and for additional strength pieces of animal sinew were glued to the back of the bow. Anthropologist Joel Janetski has written that these highly prized bows, which took a good two months to make, could drive an arrow cleanly through the body of an adult buffalo.

Bighorn are susceptible to a variety of diseases, especially during times of stress, and the fact that the animals enjoy hanging out together can cause illness to spread rapidly. Not long ago a band of sheep in the northern reaches of Yellowstone Park were infected by pinkeye, which they in turn spread to other animals during the fall rut. Rams were blinded, and several ended up falling to their deaths from cliff ledges or from the tops of the sheer, ragged pinnacles that fortify the upper reaches of the rutting grounds. By the time the disease ran its course, more than 60 percent of the herd was dead.

Just as we're about to head back to camp we catch sight of a loose band of elk heading up from the valley below through a narrow, timbered notch, bound for the long reach of meadow lying just below our camp. We set out quietly in the hopes of getting close to them, advancing carefully on the balls of our feet, walking in that slow, exaggerated way that children do when they're trying to sneak up and scare someone. But while we eventually cut a fresh line of tracks, the animals themselves are nowhere to be found. Eric and I look at each other dumbfounded, incredulous that a band of horse-sized animals could bleed into the evening shadows without so much as the scrape of a hoof or the crack of a branch.

Later, lying in my tent drifting through the cusp of sleep, my head is filled with vivid images of elk moving in and out of the forest; twice I think I hear movement outside the tent, but it is all very murky, and I cannot decide if the noise is being made by real animals, or by those walking through my imagination. It seems odd that only when sleeping outside do my dreams become clear, unadulterated mimics of the physical world that surrounds me. Out here the simple comings and goings of creatures fills much of my night, a fact that has more than once caused me to wonder if I was not somehow sensing actual events, perhaps turning a subliminal snort or the snap of a twig into mystical visions of the great creatures of the northern Rockies.

This morning dawns as fresh and full of sun as the last, and after a leisurely breakfast we load up and head south, toward Hebgen Lake. We have the choice of following a designated trail along a fourteen-mile route or shortening the distance by dropping cross-country through a series of forested ravines. We elect the overland option, not so much for the miles saved as for the sense of escapade, for the kinds of connections that are made when one treks through the mountains by map and compass. Of course there is always the chance of running into exasperating conditions—long tumbles of downed timber, boggy meadows, and young forests choked with lodgepole. But unlike the predetermined lines of a trail, the waterfalls and wildflower gardens that one stumbles across while traveling cross-country seem to carry the sheen of good fortune, of serendipity. The world off trail is by and large a delicious secret, and will return to that state in no more time than it takes for the sound of our footsteps to fade into the forest.

Of course in areas frequented by large numbers of hikers, or in especially fragile places such as certain types of alpine tundra, cross-country travel is not a good idea. But the land Eric and I find ourselves in this morning is perfect for such a foray; in fact, the stretch of pathway we intended to follow for the first two miles of the journey has seen so little use that after three hundred yards it vanishes altogether, leaving us to enact our cross-country fantasy far earlier than we had originally intended. Mature whitebark and lodgepole pines lie across the gentle slopes in loose clusters, shading lacy patches of grouse whortleberry, bluegrass, and arnica. We walk easily here, slipping quietly downward across countless game trails, and, beneath a lone lodgepole, a huge wallow where dozens of elk have been rolling in a three-inch layer of dust. Further down we stumble across a husky Douglas fir still wearing traces of an old axe blaze on its trunk, a cut that over the years has been wrapped in advancing layers of corky brown bark until today it is little more than a thin, shallow divot. Whatever trail this gash marked, perhaps a path cut back in the 1940s or 1950s to guide hunters into prime elk hunting areas, has long since been reclaimed by the woods.

Even with a good map in hand, when walking off trail I tend to quietly register the rise and fall of prominent land forms, the position of the sun, and the direction and flow of the creeks I cross. And thus I almost always "stay found." The whole notion of being lost, cast adrift in a maze of wilderness, is fascinating for the way it can throw you completely off balance, the way it can send fear racing like fire through your brain. I've seen the mere thought of being lost make people doubt the swing of a compass needle they trusted five minutes earlier, or even cause them to reshape unfamiliar surroundings into something they just know they've seen before.

Of all the people who have been lost in the Yellowstone Rockies, few stories are as revealing or compelling as that of Truman C. Everts, who was separated from the Washburn-Doane expedition on the vast, timber-strewn Central Plateau in the fall of 1870. The first night that the nearsighted Everts became separated from the rest of the party caused him no great alarm. He selected a good spot for sleeping, picketed his horse, built a fire, and went to sleep. But the next morning, when Everts dismounted to examine an opening in the dark forest, his horse bolted, taking everything but the clothes on his back, a couple of small knives, and a pair of opera glasses. It was then that "Mr. Everts' Thirty-seven days of Peril," as he would later title his harrowing story, began in earnest.

After several hours spent in a fruitless search for his horse, the taste of fear began to rise in Everts' throat, though he seemed determined to keep it from running off with his sanity. The nights were especially difficult. "I peered upward through the darkness, but all was blackness and gloom. The wind sighed mournfully through the pines. The forest seemed alive with the screeching of night birds, and angry barking of coyotes, and the prolonged, dismal howl of the gray wolf." Everts posted notices of his travel plans on several trees in a cluster of clearings, in the slim chance that friends who were out searching for him might happen upon them. When he returned the next day only to find that no one had been there, the full weight of his predicament sank in. "For the first time, I realized that I was lost. Then came a crushing sense of destitution. No food, no fire; no means to procure either; alone in an unexplored wilderness, one hundred and fifty miles from the nearest human abode, surrounded by wild beasts, and famishing with hunger."

Day after day, Everts fought like a hero to find and anchor the faith he needed to keep going. "I recollect at this time discussing the question whether there was not implanted by

Providence in every man a principle of self-preservation equal to any emergency which did not destroy his reason. I decided this question affirmatively a thousand times afterwards in my wanderings, and I record this experience here, that any person who reads it, should he ever find himself in like circumstances, may not despair. There is life in the thought."

Once, seated on the shore of Heart Lake, Everts was suddenly overjoyed to spot a large canoe approaching in the distance with a single passenger. As he paced the beach waiting for its arrival, squinting across the water, his hopes were suddenly dashed as he realized that it was nothing more than a pelican. And still the roller coaster ride of joy and horror continued. Soon after the pelican incident he was thrilled to find a patch of thistle to eat, only to be awakened from a deep sleep that same afternoon by the wailing scream of a mountain lion just a few yards off, which sent him scrambling up the nearest conifer. "I would alternately sweat and thrill with horror at the thought of being torn to pieces and devoured . . . "

A cold brew of rain and snow blew in the following morning, leading Everts to spend two long days lying under a spruce tree, doing his best to stay warm beneath thick layers of dirt and branches. When a small bird happened to land nearby, he grabbed it, plucked its feathers, and ate it raw. He later found a patch of warm ground in a thermal area where he camped for seven days, during which time there fell a foot of snow. On the third night Everts broke through the thin crust of earth above the boiling springs while he was sleeping, severely scalding his hip; this injury, combined with his frostbitten feet, which were already starting to fester, would cause terrific pain during the remainder of his ordeal.

As the days passed, necessity brought leaps of invention. One afternoon Everts realized that the lens from his opera glasses could be used to start fires. He also unraveled the threads from a linen handkerchief to mend his clothes, used a piece of tape and a pin from his coat to fashion a fishing line (it never worked), and, cutting the tops of his boots off and sewing up one side, turned them into pouches for carrying food. Thus equipped, he left the thermal area, by now almost certain that his friends had given up searching for him. "I know that from this time onward to the day of my rescue, my mind, though unimpaired in those perceptions needful to self preservation, was in a condition to receive impressions akin to insanity. I was constantly traveling in dreamland, and indulging in strange reveries such as I had never before known." Thus Everts existed in a kind of bizarre duality, one side marked by attention to the needs of survival, and the other by strange forays into the depths of fantasy. "Thus I lived in a world of ideal happiness, and in a world of positive suffering at the same time."

Carefully studying his options for escape, Everts finally decided on the shortest route possible, which involved heading back to Yellowstone Lake and scaling the high peaks to the west, making for the settlements on the Madison River Valley. But after two days of rugged searching, not to mention a night when his shelter caught fire and badly burned him, Everts began to realize that there was no easy pass across the mountains. The only other option left to him was to return the way the party came, along the Yellowstone River, through the horrors of rugged canyons and thickets and vast, dark forests littered with thousands and thousands of acres of downed timber. Just as he was about to commit to yet another day of searching for a route across the mountains, the apparition of an old friend suddenly appeared before him, instructing him to "go back immediately, as rapidly as your strength will permit."

By now Everts had lost all sense of time, and spent most nights dreaming of the best restaurants in New York and Washington, each filled with enormous tables of pies and oyster stews. The upper and lower falls of the Yellowstone, which had inspired him nearly to the point of rapture when he first spied them with the Washburn party, he now described as enemies that had lured him to destruction. His spirit friend finally disappeared, and was replaced by talking arms and legs. Game animals were plentiful, but with no means of killing them they were little more than an aggravation; at Tower Falls Everts spent an entire half-day trying to catch a single grasshopper.

Finally, thirty-seven days after he had been separated from his party near the shore of Yellowstone Lake, two searchers found Everts in a ravine near Blacktail Deer Creek. Their dog picked up a scent, which the men assumed was that of a bear. In fact, from a distance one of the searchers—a colorful character by the name of Yellowstone Jack—was certain enough that the dark, prostrate lump he saw in the distance was a bear that he very nearly raised his gun and fired. "It never occurred to me that it was Everts," wrote Jack. "I went up close to the object; it was making a low groaning noise, crawling along upon its knees and elbows, trying to drag itself up the mountain."

"Are you Mr. Everts?" Jack asked the bony wisp of a man with no shoes, who now weighed little more than seventy pounds.

"Yes," said Everts. "All that is left of him."

Everts was unable to digest food, so one of the men grabbed his horse and dashed off to Fort Ellis, seventy miles distant, to procure medicine to help restore his system. As Everts lay in the Turkey Pen Cabin, by now in excruciating pain and very close to death, a salty old hunter happened by. When he heard of Everts' digestion problem he ran out the door, grabbed a sack of bear fat, and quickly rendered it into a pint of oil for Everts to drink. By the next day Everts was out of pain, and filled with the deep, hollow ring of an appetite. The ordeal was finally over.

As we approach Cub Creek, approximately three miles from where we started our bushwhacking, the amount of downed timber begins to increase significantly, leaving us to scramble over, around, and under a hodgepodge of fallen trees—a task made considerably more difficult by the fifty-pound packs strapped to our backs. Fortunately these conditions don't last for long, and in another half mile we amble out onto the Axolotl Lake trail, barely two hundred yards west of the point we were aiming for. Resting in a beautiful meadow flushed with the lavender blooms of sticky geranium, I pull out the topos to review our options for routes to Cabin Creek. If we head west a short ways on this path and then bushwhack southward for just under a mile, we can save nearly three miles. Furthermore, the longer route traverses the south foot of Skyline Ridge, which is already starting to broil under the midday sun; going cross-country will keep us in the shade of the conifers, and never more than a stone's throw from the cool, southbound waters of Cub Creek.

We head into this last leg of bushwhacking with fresh memories of this morning's overland trek, which, for the most part, was little more than a walk in the park. But fifty yards off the path, it becomes painfully obvious that this will be an adventure of a far different sort. The land is riddled with downed timber and steep-sided ravines, and in places is thoroughly choked with thick clusters of young lodgepole, their branches grabbing our feet and slapping at our arms and faces as we pass. We try a variety of strategies. One of these involves actually walking on top of the massive jumbles of logs, jerking our bodies from side to side to maintain balance under the weight of the packs, trying our best to avoid being pulled into the snarls of sharp stubs and broken branches that lie below.

Weary of this tightrope action, I decide to make my way over to the edge of the stream gorge, which at this point consists of a fifty-degree slope of highly eroded soil, the upper reaches lying roughly seventy feet above the creek itself. While the footing is precarious, I'm able to make progress by dashing from one shrub or dwarf lodgepole pine to the next, grabbing the bases of the branches while trying to kick in a toehold with the edge of my boots. It isn't pretty, but for a time this dash-and-grab method seems like a tremendous improvement over the tortuous traverse in the thick of the forest. An improvement, that is, until I come to a forty-yard stretch of hard-packed dirt, with no vegetation at all but for a few paltry clumps of snakeweed, their branches frail enough to be pulled up by the slightest tug.

And so here is one of those classic dilemmas. Do I attempt the crossing, knowing full well that a fall could mean a high-speed, seventy-foot slide into the jumble of rocks that line Cub Creek? Or do I struggle back over the lip of the gorge and resume the tiresome plod through that hodgepodge of fallen logs? The crossing would be much easier if I could kick into the slope to gain purchase, but the surface is just too hard. If I'm to keep any measure of boot tread on the ground, it will mean holding my feet at acute angles to the hill.

In the end I decide to risk the crossing, primarily because I'm wearing heavy, stiff-collared leather boots that greatly fortify my ankles. It is every bit as precarious as I imagined, and soon I find myself contemplating the terrain with the intensity of a person scanning the ground for a lost contact lens, trying my best to avoid any small, round rocks that might kick out from under me if stepped on. When I do go forward, it is much less a clean, conscious act than a move to regain my fizzling sense of balance. After what seems like thirty minutes, but is probably no more than two, I finally make it across the slope, lunging for a fistful of juniper with one hand just as my trailing foot leaves the hard pack. Sadly, my feeling of relief is shortlived. Fifty yards farther the slope becomes an outright cliff, something a teenage mountain goat wouldn't try, and I am once again forced back into the forest.

Walking continues to be less than enjoyable for the remainder of the bushwhack, and when we finally stumble into the Cabin Creek drainage I wear several cuts and scrapes on my legs, the majority of which were gathered in the last two hundred yards, when I found myself stumbling and slashing through a dense braid of young trees. By comparison, the more mature forest growing in the Cabin Creek canyon, a loose toss of timber and shrubs, seems like the Garden of Eden. Now on the home stretch, we stop for a long, cool drink under a stately lodgepole. Looking up through its branches, I can't help but think about what this spot must have looked like seventy years ago, when in all likelihood this particular tree was just one of hundreds of lodgepole huddled here branch to branch, tight as the bristles on a hairbrush, pushing ever upward in a race for the sky.

The tenacious, sun-worshiping lodgepole is a kind of trademark of the West, having laid claim to more than a million square miles from Alaska to New Mexico. True to the name given it by Lewis and Clark, the tree was indeed an essential part of lodge construction for many Native American peoples. Women from various tribes cut hundreds of two- to three-inch diameter lodgepole late each spring, stripped the bark, and then put them aside to season through the arid summer. By autumn the poles would weigh barely seven pounds apiece, yet be remarkably strong and resistant to cracking. Fifteen lashed together at one end with strips of hide and spread into an upright cone made the perfect frame on which to lay the thick, coarse hides that would help stay the sting of a northern winter.

It didn't take the Europeans long to catch on. Lodgepole not only fenced many a cowboy's first corral, but they also shored up gold mine shafts at Bannock, Cripple Creek, and Virginia City. And it was the lodgepole that great teams of lumberjacks cut, trimmed, and split each winter, to be floated downriver in the spring for use as cross ties on the first Rocky Mountain railroads.

What allows the lodgepole to carry happily on in the face of an event like the fires of '88 is that in every stand are a number of "fire pines"—trees bearing cones with scales glued so tightly together with resin that nothing but the hot blast of a forest fire can pop them open. And thus the very thing that devastates the forest is also the thing that releases the seeds of the next generation. There are places in this region where a hundred thousand seedlings are sprouting on a single acre of burned ground. As the years turn round, each little tree will race for the sun, jockeying for position like kids worming to the curb before the start of a parade. So close do the trees grow together that if one weakens and then breaks in the wind, more than likely it will never reach the ground.

Cabin Creek leads us out of the mountains through a corridor washed with raspberry, silky phacelia, fireweed, thimbleberry, strawberry, false Solomonseal, and Oregon grape. Two miles from where we came out of the brush, the canyon suddenly pinches off against the northern prow of Boat Mountain, a volcanic monolith rising two thousand feet from the creek waters in just two or three staggering leaps. The stream licks and roils at the charcoal-colored foot of the mountain, which over the years has been polished to a smooth luster; from here I can see the bright colors of geranium and paintbrush blooms nodding against the dark, marbled panes of the chasm wall.

By three o'clock we've reached the trailhead, located at a small campground just off of Hebgen Lake. Several families are in various stages of picnicking, kids giggling and swatting at their siblings with hot-dog sticks, and running through fields of fireweed with black Labradors and English setters in tow, the dogs so happy as to be on the edge of deliriousness. Upon our approach, dogs, children, even a parent in the middle of a hamburger flip, stop in their tracks and stare; two boys playing around the water pump move shoulder to shoulder and start whispering to each other, neither willing to take his eyes off us. It isn't as if they perceive us as threatening, merely strange. One little boy wears a look that I last saw on *Saturday Night Live*, when that average American family rang the doorbell of their neighbor's house, only to find themselves face to face with the Coneheads.

There were in fact several times on my treks through the region when adults and children alike would pass me on a trail, ask me where I was going, and then shake their heads in utter disbelief that anyone would walk so far with a pack on his back. (Most outfitters were equally incredulous, but then most of them have long believed that if God would have wanted us to walk, he wouldn't have made horses.) The fact is that in a great many places backpacking has slowed dramatically; in the national park system alone overnight stays in the backcountry have dropped by more than 35 percent in the past fifteen years.

I used to attribute this to the fact that the baby boomers' children were just too young to hit the trail; once they reached twelve or thirteen, I reasoned, then backpacking would see a major rebound. Not so. The fact is that most people no longer have the time available to spend even two or three days on a trail. I recall being in sociology classes in the late 1970s, and hearing my professors making blue sky predictions about how leisure time would increase dramatically in the coming decades. But as countless studies are showing, free time is diminishing under an onslaught of domestic and work-related demands. Juliet Schor of Harvard notes that when you add up the number of hours that people spend over the course of a year working on the job and at home, it amounts to a full month more than what it was twenty years ago. A report by R. H. Bruskin Associates says that the average American now spends thirteen hours of the weekend in chores, doing things like cleaning, shopping, cooking, and paying bills.

This is not the way the rest of the world works. The typical American who's been on the job five years can count on eleven official holidays and twelve days of paid vacation. Contrast that to Europeans, who on average are given more than twice as many days off—not as a measure of seniority, mind you, but as a basic job benefit. While the industrious Japanese don't tend to take all the time off available to them, they're actually allotted 30 percent more of it than Americans. Time for free-form exploration, for not just traveling to a place but slowing down enough to savor it, has become so rare as to be an anomaly.

Businesses are springing up in most Rocky Mountain vacation towns that specialize in personalized travel itineraries. With only a few precious days to spend, people are more determined than ever to make sure that everything is as perfect as possible. There's no longer any room in the schedule for a bad meal, a missed airplane connection, delays at the car rental counter, or the occasional lousy room. When I was writing nature/travel guides, the key concern of marketing people was that the books offer places to go within an hour or two of major urban areas—places "highly accessible," as one publicist put it, "to the vast majority of people, who can barely manage an afternoon off."

In the foreseeable future, we seem destined to continue to take most of our nature in symbol more than fact, eyeballing it from our living rooms via the Discovery Channel, or crooning over it every December as we rip open our Ansel Adams Christmas cards. While twenty years ago we heard much about loving the wild places to death—a fact that most certainly still threatens some areas—these days I worry more about whether or not America's precious wild heritage, having started to drift out of touch, will also drift out of mind.

SEVEN

Just west of Yellowstone National Park, at the foot of the stirring parapets of the Madison Range, is the Hebgen Valley, catch basin for the clear, cold waters of the Madison River. It was here in 1959 that one of the most astonishing earthquakes in the history of the Rockies occurred, rattling six hundred thousand square miles of land stretching from North Dakota all the way to western Washington. During the main part of the tremor the water in ten-mile-long Hebgen Lake started sloshing back and forth as if a child were rocking a dishpan, sending enormous waves crashing over the top of the massive earthen dam on the west end of the reservoir. In Yellowstone National Park several new fissures opened, and nearly three hundred springs and geysers erupted simultaneously, more than half of which no one had ever seen erupt before. Indeed, had you been up and about in that particular portion of the park, mud volcanoes belching and nearly every thermal area spewing great volumes of water, some making odd whistling noises in the process, it may well have seemed the grand finale for nothing less than the end of the world. In Billings, 150 miles to the east, the local newspaper reported that immediately following the quake a man staggered out of a bar on Montana Street, swearing never to drink again; at the same time, another patron who had just left the bar ran back in and demanded a double. The next day, in West Yellowstone, Mae Hill hung a sign on the office door of her Yellowstone Lodge and Trailer Court: "Left for Ogden, Utah at 9:15 A.M. Tuesday, 18th of August. P.S. Will come back when quake stops."

But the quake itself wasn't the only show of force to be reckoned with on that warm August night. Just downstream from Cabin Creek, more than 80 million tons of rock—enough to cover the entire island of Manhattan in two feet of rubble—shook loose from a 1,300-foot high mountain face and careened into the Madison River at speeds nearing one hundred miles per hour. The slide had so much force behind it that the leading edge rose more than three hundred feet up the slope on the opposite side of the valley. Twenty-eight vacationers were killed; of those, only nine were ever found.

Of all the dramas spun out along the Madison River that night, perhaps none is more shocking than the tale of the Bennett family, of Coeur d'Alene, Idaho. Awakened by the great roar of the rock face as it let loose from the other side of the canyon, Mrs. Bennett and her husband hurried out of their camper to check on their four children, who were sleeping nearby. Before either knew what was happening, they were hit with a tremendous blast of wind pushing out in front of the slide. Mrs. Bennett watched in utter disbelief as her husband grabbed for a small conifer to steady himself, was picked off his feet and twisted like a flag in a tempest, and then, when he could hold on no longer, blew away down the canyon, never to be seen alive again. Less than a minute later she watched in horror as one of her children flew past, followed by an empty car rolling by in great thuds and groans, not thirty feet away. Shortly thereafter she was knocked unconscious and washed into the river by huge waves of water thundering down the canyon. At dawn the next morning, nearly six hours after the nightmare began, she and her sixteen-year-old son Philip were found by searchers, the only two of their family of six to survive. As was common to those having endured this ordeal, they were naked, the fierce winds and waves having ripped every shred of clothing from their bodies.

The quake had a profound effect on Yellowstone's thermal features. In Biscuit Basin, beautiful Sapphire Pool, which before the event had offered only modest gurgles and bursts of steam bubbles, had by the next day become a full-fledged geyser, spewing cloudy water eight feet into the air. Three days later the eruptions became violent, tearing one-hundred-pound chunks of geyserite from the rims and tossing them fifty feet from the edge of the crater. Elsewhere, Cascade and Economic geysers started up again after having been dormant for forty years. The Giantess Geyser, which had been so thoroughly ogled by the Washburn Expedition of 1870, launched into an unprecedented eruption that lasted for more than a hundred hours. Many other geysers went into shorter eruptive intervals for the remainder of the year, while Old Faithful— somewhat erratic the day after the quake—eventually settled into a schedule that averaged five and a half minutes slower than before. Generally, temperatures in the thermal springs of Yellowstone rose about six degrees after the 1959 quake, while discharge increased by roughly 10 percent.

Most of the world's active earthquake zones correspond to the outer borders of seven mammoth plates that make up the earth's outer shell—seventy-mile-thick pieces of a jigsaw puzzle floating on a sea of liquid magma, drifting like hunks of skin on a pot of boiling chocolate pudding. These plates are constantly moving toward or away from each other, or, in the case of California's San Andreas Fault, grinding past one another at a rate of several inches per year.

Curiously, the particular seismic belt that stretches south out of Montana through Yellowstone National Park near the Idaho-Wyoming border, through Utah along the front of the Wasatch Range, and finally into southern Nevada, is one of only a few active earthquake zones in the world that doesn't parallel a boundary between two tectonic plates. Its dynamics are little understood. But seeing the massive fault scarps that now line the Hebgen Valley, or sitting on the shores of Quake

Lake, where just thirty-five years ago there was no lake at all, one can hardly help but wonder when the earth will move again.

In the immediate vicinity of the 1959 quake, eight thousand to ten thousand shocks are still recorded every year—fully 1 percent of the number logged worldwide. The Old Faithful Visitor Center may track up to a hundred small tremors in a single day. In October of 1935, the city of Helena experienced more than seven hundred tremors; four months later, just when residents thought the rock and roll show was really over, the ground started shaking again, causing some politicians to suggest that the capitol be moved elsewhere.

I've entered the park alone from the west, near Gneiss Creek, and will travel along a route that angles southeast for roughly fifteen miles, ending on the Madison River at Seven Mile Bridge. There is not a single hiker on the path, one reason being that most of it passes forests badly blackened or turned to rust in the 1988 fires, and another because heavy grizzly activity has led park officials to restrict the area to day use only. My plan is to rendezvous with Jane and friends on the Madison in late afternoon, spend the night with them amidst the great summer sardine huddle of Madison Campground, and then begin a forty-mile stretch of trail out of Old Faithful the following morning.

Despite the fact that the Gneiss Creek Trail now brushes elbows with an almost endless reach of burn, I decide early on that I like it. For much of its length it is one of those skinny, hardly used trails barely two boot-widths across, and in grassy areas, it can't be found at all; indeed, the bison path I cross two miles into the trek is twice as wide and far more heavily used than this one.

Paths in Yellowstone are marked not by slashes cut into trees, as has long been the practice in other areas, but by small orange metal tags fastened high up on the trunks. Many times in burned areas like this one the trees that held the tags have either blown over or turned to ashes, or the bright orange paint that once covered them has been reduced to the same blackened char that coats the adjacent tree. Had I not brought binoculars, I'd be spending a good deal of my time wandering around looking for the route. Far from being a major problem, though, such conditions tend to lend a bit of spice to the journey, giving breath to the illusion that I am stumbling around completely unfettered through the backcountry of one of the greatest national parks in the world.

The biggest reason I like the Gneiss Creek Trail is that it provides opportunities for engaging in conversations with the locals, most especially hawks, great blue herons, and sandhill cranes. Three miles into the walk, strolling through a rather mystical-looking place thick with blackened pine and spindly quilts of fireweed, a Swainson's hawk suddenly drops over the hummocks to the north and lands in a tree not thirty yards off the trail. He watches me, letting out long, raspy whistles that cut like sirens through the hot summer air. We stare at each other for a while, and when I start to move again, he moves with me, floating from tree to tree with slow, deliberate sweeps of his gray- and ivory-colored wings. Each time before liftoff his call changes to a laughing, sputtering shriek, as if he were drunk on the notion of thousands of small mammals running through these thick weaves of grass, where three years ago there was only forest. He flies just ahead of me for so long, calls down to me from the ghost trees so many times beyond what I would normally expect from a mere male territorial display, that I start to feel like Carlos Castaneda trying to divine the meaning of a crow's antics in the deserts of Mexico.

Swainson's hawks are fast, beautiful fliers that can often be seen tracing low zigzags across open ground before suddenly dropping like a shot to nab their prey. Though they are far from shy when it comes to defending their nests (some females seem perfectly willing to get within ten feet of an intruding human), these birds will nonetheless commonly lose eggs to marauding crows, and their young to attacks by great horned owls. One of the most remarkable aspects of the Swainson's life is its migration behavior. In the fall flocks of the south-bound hawks will flow together like braids of a stream, until several thousand birds are traveling together, a river of wings bound for the soft, dry warmth of Argentina.

Soon after my hawk friend finally peels away from the trail, a huge chorus of ravens crank up their voices, sounding like a pack of blues singers who just swallowed their cigarettes. Though one or two pause to look my way, in general they are much too involved in goading one another to pay much attention to me, their squawking bundles of black feathers flapping up and settling quickly back down again, as if their feet had been tethered to the branches. Beyond the wave of cackling I can also hear the sound of a snipe diving through the air like a kamikaze, his wings whistling in faster and faster pulses as he hurtles toward the meadows below.

The best bird act of the day, however, is the third one. I've heard sandhill cranes calling in the distance almost since I left the trailhead, and now a pair slips out of the sky like God's own airline, coming to rest right beside me in a long meadow choked with yarrow, sage, and pale agoseris. These birds too come surprisingly close, especially if this is their feeding ground, and quickly set to stabbing at various bugs and roots, following me like a couple of farm geese all the way down the length of the meadow. Much as I might like to attribute this behavior to curiosity, more than likely the birds are simply protecting what is theirs—keeping an eye on me, like the stern, white-haired women in my hometown who paced their porches after school, making sure that no kids played on their fences or threw candy wrappers in their freshly raked yards.

There are few sounds in all of nature as pleasant as that sweet, wild chortle of the sandhill crane. It is the mountain meadow equivalent of the loon, though without the shades of deliriousness, a kind of archetypal timbre of the wilderness. Besides this beautiful call, the most delightful aspect of sand-hills is their dance. Using their long, spindly legs like pogo sticks, the birds will catapult themselves six, ten, even fifteen feet into the air, wings slightly outspread, and then settle back to the ground again, often following this with several graceful bows. Sometimes the birds will start these movements by first tossing a root or even a clod of dirt into the air. While there may be only one or two birds dancing in a given place, at other times things can unfold like a scene from a junior prom, where those standing around looking on at one or two dancers suddenly decide to get into the action themselves, until the entire group is bouncing up and down in the meadows like so many brown feathered balls. While crane dancing is usually thought of in relation to spring courtship, it in fact occurs in virtually every season of the year.

Some sandhills breed as far north as coastal Alaska, Siberia, and the central Canadian Arctic. These more northerly birds will start coming together in loose groups during the latter part of August. By late September or early October they have generally left the north country, flying day and night, most headed for the southwestern United States or nothern Mexico, three thousand to four thousand miles distant.

As this handsome pair of sandhills finally abandons me to the forest, I can hear at least two other pairs singing somewhere to the south; when the birds who were with me join in, the air seems suddenly filled with the sound, as if all the valleys in all the park were on this particular day the exclusive domain of the sandhill. It's hard to imagine that forty or fifty years ago it was not unheard of for spring concentrations of sandhills in Nebraska or Montana to reach thirty thousand or even forty thousand birds. In 1945 researcher W. J. Breckenridge reported a fabulous encounter with upwards of twenty thousand cranes near the confluence of the North Platte and South Platte Rivers. "The flock peeled up off the ground in a clamorous tumult and the cranes literally filled the air with their huge beating wings. Gradually the clamoring mass of birds rose higher and higher toward the massive white cumulus clouds floating in the deep blue sky. And as they rose they slowly began to organize themselves into a huge circling whirlpool-like formation that turned ever so slowly and all the while towering higher and higher. Their calls gradually became less and less distinct and their huge forms smaller and smaller until finally the highest bird had to be followed with 8x binoculars or they would be lost to sight. At this point the sky seemed covered by layer after layer of circling cranes, with always a higher stratum beyond . . . " Sadly, most of us will never know such a sight, since populations of sandhills have dwindled dramatically as their nesting habitat has been sacrificed to development.

The trail turns south now, weaving through mile after mile of dead timber and western wheatgrass. Though the time will come when I tire of walking through burned lands, it occurs to me that firescapes are at their most disagreeable when you're short of time, when you've come to inhale as much green earth as you can manage in a few precious days of vacation. With more than three hundred miles of walking yet to go, for now I take the burn in stride, taking time to pull back the weave of fireweed, harebells, groundsel, and lupine to discover the tiny needled heads of lodgepole seedlings launching the next hundred years of forest. One drawback to the burn, however, is that with the loss of trees there is no longer a curtain of branches to block sounds; with a bit of west wind blowing, the thin purr of cars running up and down Highway 191 drifts easily across the flats. But even that fades by the time I reach Maple Creek, which is pouring through this strange, sunburnt land with barely a sound, running past the thin shadows of the ghost trees, and countless purple spatters of lupine.

Abundant moisture this year has turned a significant portion of these lands—burned and otherwise—into a wonderful collection of wildflower gardens. One of the most striking of these is a vast reach of blue flax cradling the trail, their delicate blooms washed in that weightless, hopeful color of a June sky. It's rather uncommon to see this flower in great quantity, and yet here are hundreds and hundreds of them, hanging from the tips of branches so slender that they dance and sway even when there is no apparent breeze. As delicate as these branches appear, however, they are woven with the same tough, stringy fibers common to cultivated flax—the very fibers that Egyptians used to wrap their dead, and Native

Americans relied on to make everything from rope to fishing line.

Off in the distance, through long lines of dead trees, I can see a fine six-point elk cantering to the west, appearing and then disappearing from view, melding into grass and then emerging from it, a Bev Doolittle canvas come to life. Shortly afterward, near Cougar Creek, I spot a thin line of dark brown hair moving behind a veneer of chest-high grass, and my mind instantly turns it into the spine of a grizzly. Curiously, I am not alarmed. I stop and loosen my pack belt, as I've done in my mind countless times before, spot a tree that looks climbable, and wait quietly. When a head finally pops up it belongs not to a bear but to an enormous bull elk; spotting me, he thunders off through the burn like a freight train, the sounds of his hoofs pounding against the dirt lingering on long after I lose sight of him.

I'm very near the east-west line of the Bannock, or Great Trail, as it was sometimes called, a two-hundred-mile-long braid of Native American pathways now all but vanished beneath a tumble of conifers, whortleberry, sage, and grasses. Though it was probably in use for only forty years, for more than half of that time this was the stuff that unruffled nomadic visions were made of, a safe corridor over which the Bannocks could travel eastward from their homes on the Snake River Plains to access vast herds of bison still roaming the swells of the high plains.

The Bannocks' ancestral home included the camas meadows and prairies of southern and eastern Idaho. This region had no lack of food, especially when it came to that key staple, the camas, whose deep blue flowers formed such thick blankets across the land that some early explorers, looking out from some high promontory, at first mistook the coloring for lakes. The Bannocks supplemented their camas diet with a variety of other plants and berries, as well as with plentiful supplies of fish. But by the late 1830s, one highly valued component of their lives, the bison, had already started to dwindle, the result of overharvesting by both Native Americans and the white trappers who'd been roaming this country for twenty years. Forced to either give up the meat, tipi skins, and robes which they so favored, or venture into the hinterlands to the east to acquire them, the Bannocks, already adept at nomadic living, chose the latter.

The decision of how to reach the bison was not a difficult one. Accessing them via a northern route was by far the easiest and shortest of the choices, but would have carried them into the land of their fierce enemies, the Blackfeet. Reaching the herds by going east over Teton Pass and through Gros Ventre Valley to the Wind River Plains was not only an extremely rugged journey, but it too held the chance for unpleasant encounters with neighboring tribes. Not that the Bannocks necessarily shunned conflicts. But early summer was not a time they considered appropriate for war. What's more, going for bison meant traveling in small, highly mobile groups— hardly the kind of organization with which to do battle. Thus the most logical path was across the northern range of what would one day become Yellowstone National Park—a route that offered not only ample supplies of wood, food, and water, but also of obsidian, a shiny, black volcanic glass used to fashion the tools needed for skinning and preparing meat and hides. Furthermore, the shaping of those tools was for the most part done with elk antlers, which could also be found here in great abundance.

Members of other tribes, including Flathead, Lemhi, and Fort Hall Shoshone also used this travel corridor on occasion, but at least until the late 1860s, the Yellowstone country never seemed better suited to any people than it did to the Bannock. As the tribe was shuffled onto reservations, Indian agents tried to discourage the people from making their seasonal treks along the Great Trail—a request that may have been better received had the reservations held something for them other than hunger and starvation. By 1878, the seasonal customs of the early days crumbling about them, the last of the Bannocks made their way across the meadows and mountains of Yellowstone.

When park officials set about laying out a road to connect

Mammoth with the town of Cooke City, they chose a route
that closely followed the Bannock Trail. Today there are several places where you can still see remains of Bannock camps,
many littered with obsidian flakes, or even scars on the ground
laid down by horse-drawn travois. To stumble across such
things while walking through the silence of the backcountry
can be a powerful experience—each scar, each chip of stone
a window into the most stirring of lives and times, now broken
and scattered to the winds.

When the timber along this trail was devoured by the fires of
1988, the shade of course went with it. The full force of July's
heat now pours onto the land, simmering my skin, sucking
moisture out of me almost as fast as I can pour it back down
my throat. Though conditions are decidedly uncomfortable,
I'm trying my best to bask in this wash of heat; in a pitifully
few short weeks the sun will have rolled away, pushed southward by the cold breath of autumn.

Shimmering in the heat on the open, slanted brows of the
moraines are dense patches of lupine—great washes of indigo-
colored blooms lying like pieces of fallen sky against the
brown faces of the hills. The color is even more dramatic when
it rises next to fields of ivory-colored yarrow, which in places
run fifty or sixty yards out from the edges of the lupine. The
trail hugs these blooms until almost a mile out from the Madison River, at which point it plunges into a forest of young
burned lodgepole, pubescent ghost trees standing up to their
shins in fields of yellowing forbs.

Having walked for fifteen miles without seeing so much as
one other person, Madison Campground, filled to the brim as
it is every night from late June through Labor Day, is at first
quite a shock. Children scream with delight as they chase one
another across the park lands that cradle the Madison River.
Fathers, some clearly new to the art of fishing, fix lures on
the lines of spinning rods for their sons, doing so with all the
sobriety and purposefulness of a deacon preparing the altar
for Sunday service. Couples of every shape and size stroll
through the loose weave of conifers: young marrieds, laughing

and pushing against each other's shoulders, and older partners hand in hand, pausing here and there to watch Steller's
jays flit about the conifers. "Do you want hot dogs or ham-
burgers tonight?" a mother calls out from an adjacent campsite to her children; it's a choice they clearly consider to be
a win-win situation. On the other side of the road a blonde
seven-year-old girl dressed in faded yellow shorts and a green
tank top smudged with dirt, rushes into camp, hand in hand
with a new friend. "This is Monica," she announces. "We're
going to look at the river!" Two boys cruise the campground
loops on purple stingrays, pulling wheelies whenever the
mood strikes; by the third time around the loop they've joined
forces with another boy, and soon afterward, find three more.
Snippets of conversations drift through the air like wood
smoke. "We've seen Old Faithful three times, and we're going
again in the morning . . ." "If you're taking the twins swimming, I'm going fishing with John . . ." "Kevin, did you and
your brother eat the chocolate bars I bought for the s'mores?"

This, and not trekking through the backcountry kibitzing
with sandhill cranes, is the usual Yellowstone experience. It
is a portable society, an eager clan of strangers all in uncom-
monly good moods—friendly, smiling, a nomadic carnival
drunk on the possibilities of summer vacation. When I first
started car camping on my own, I was amazed at the number
of people who, coming into a nearly empty campground,
would set up right beside me, as if there were still some comfort to be had from circling the wagons before nightfall. Indeed, I believe that were it possible for every family visiting
Yellowstone to have its own secluded campsite miles from
the nearest other human, the majority would still prefer to
live in the suburbs of places like Madison Campground. Yellowstone, its campgrounds buzzing with activity, its roads
choked with people abandoning their cars, sprinting off to
film elk and bison like Dith Pran dashing through the streets
of Phnom Penh, in many ways remains the quintessential
Western vacation.

I used to think that the first recreational travelers to Yellowstone were wrapped in the kinds of trappings found on

Northern Pacific Railroad coaches rolling west out of Minnesota. Seats were comfortable, trains were on time, and the food—everything from fresh Atlantic oysters to strawberry Mary Ann—was very good. After dinner you might order a glass of Bulgarian milk and curl up with the St. Paul paper or a copy of the *Atlantic*, and then an hour or two later, toddle off to your Pullman car for a good night's sleep. (A note at the bottom of an 1897 rate schedule says with no small measure of confidence: "Comment on the Pullman Car service is unnecessary.")

But the truth is that this kind of cushy traveling ended when you reached Livingston. The branch railroad from Livingston to Cinnabar, which was located just north of Gardiner, was the first clue to travelers that some kind of change was underfoot. Writing in *The Nation* about a trip he made to Yellowstone in 1887, H. T. Finck disparages the spur line out of Livingston. "For slowness," he complains, "it would certainly get the first prize at a national exhibition of timetables." At one point the train stopped for ten minutes so that the engineer could leave a box of merchandise in the middle of a field, and pick up a bucket of buttermilk for the crew and passengers. "Shortly afterwards the train was again stopped, apparently because the engineer espied a couple of prairie chickens on the hillside. He pursued them with his revolver, bagged one of them, and the train stubbornly proceeded to its destination, notwithstanding the polite request of one of the passengers to the conductor to wait until he had caught a string of trout in the adjacent Yellowstone River." A week later, when Finck was returning over the same road, he tells of stopping for fifteen minutes "while conductor, engineer, and brakeman amused themselves with a game of base-ball."

At Cinnabar visitors left the train and climbed aboard stagecoaches, which then took them on five- or six-day treks through the park to Mammoth, the Upper and Lower Geyser Basins, Yellowstone Lake, and the Grand Canyon of the Yellowstone. Some stayed in hotels along the way, while many others opted for tent camps. Among the latter was a woman named M. A. Cruikshank, who in 1883 writes in some detail of the difficulties she and her party encountered almost as soon as they entered the park. "At the steepest places we got out and walked: and then began our sufferings. The dirt was almost ankle deep and the heat and clarity of the air made it a serious business. This may be laid down as certain: wherever you go there are streams to ford, corduroy to fall over, sage-brush plains to crawl along and mountains to cross. The strong can stand it, and enjoy it; but it is no place for the delicate. Even the strong would be satisfied with less of it. I never longed for railroads as I did there."

Later that night Ms. Cruikshank and five other women ended up spending the night crammed into a tent with fifteen men, including one army officer who was a relentless snorer. (The next morning, when someone compared the snoring man to a geyser, one woman strongly disagreed. "Oh, a geyser is decent—it only goes off once an hour; he has kept it up all night forty times a minute.") For pillows the women were offered burlap sacks filled with potatoes. Waking the next morning and being somewhat dismayed to find that there were no toilet facilities, Cruikshank was advised by an Englishwoman to "shake yourself off like a donkey—that is all you can do."

And there was always the occasional surprise. In 1910 two stage drivers tied on a bad whisky drunk and decided to ride toward West Yellowstone to trash a camp full of tourists. This little wrecking operation had barely gotten underway when the screams of several women brought the camp manager— a big man named Ralph Knight—running to the scene. Knight went over to the drivers, gave two terrific swings of his big right hand, and knocked both of them out. No sooner had they hit the wood floor of the platform tent than Ralph noticed the dump wagon passing by with a full load of horse droppings from the barn; as the tourists looked on in utter amazement, Knight halted the wagon, picked up the unconscious men and tossed them into the bed of manure, and then waved the driver on to the dump.

Another time, on a warm summer morning in late July of

1914, a dashing robber named Edwin Trafton managed to hold up nineteen stages full of tourists on a twisted stretch of road near Shoshone Lake. Trafton was a convicted felon to whom the U.S. government had for some reason given the job of carrying mail through the region, and thus had intimate knowledge of the roads in the western part of the park. He put that information to use in choosing the perfect place for unleashing what his own grandson called "the most brazen robbery in the history of stagecoach travel in America."

North of Shoshone Lake the main stage road of the day made a steep climb up a small hill. As was common in several places in the park, passengers were asked to get out and help the horses by pushing the stage up the incline. From the top of the hill the driver would then proceed down the other side, leaning hard into the foot brake to keep from running into the backs of the horses' legs, finally stopping in a small hollow for passengers to reboard. Once he'd driven out of the hollow, the driver would then sound a small trumpet as a signal to the next stage in line that it was okay to start up the hill. Trafton simply stood at the downslope and caught each person as he or she walked down the road, instructing each with rifle in hand to dump wallets and jewelry into an open blanket. As he finished with each group, he instructed the driver to pull off the road into a meadow and blow the horn, and then waited for the next batch of tourists to arrive. It was finally the driver of the twentieth stage, a man named Bill Frazier, who got suspicious of the unusually long delay, walked up to the top of the hill, and spotted the robbery in progress. Frazier ran back, warned the drivers of the other twenty-one stages, and then turned his rig around to lead a mad dash back to West Yellowstone.

Despite a major effort to apprehend him, Trafton made an easy getaway. When the authorities finally did catch up to him a year later, it was only because his wife, angry at an affair Trafton was having with a neighbor woman, decided to spill the beans to the sheriff about where he was hiding out.

Yet for most Yellowstone tourists, the strange events they encountered or heard about along the way never seemed to diminish their enthusiasm for the place. Despite the annoyances of dust and snoring army men, Ms. Cruikshank waxes poetic about the park in her diary. Upon seeing Yellowstone Falls, she and her traveling companions conclude that "earth could not furnish another such beautiful sight." By the time she rounds the last bend of the road out of the park she's already vowing to return, the next time staying longer, "until I'm satisfied." As for all of those inconveniences that seemed to test her during the first days of her journey, well, those were inconsequential potholes on the road to adventure. "When one surrenders oneself in good faith to the wilderness," she boldly declares at the end of her journey, "the decencies of civilized life become almost impertinences."

The cost of the tour that led to Ms. Cruikshank's grand shift in perspective was thirty-five dollars. Add to this approximately fifty dollars for round-trip fare from Minneapolis on the Northern Pacific, and seven dollars more for a half-section on a Pullman car, and the cost of the vacation comes very close to a hundred dollars (over $1,500 in today's money), substantially more than many families could afford.

What's amazing is that so many people who didn't have that kind of money to spend still wanted to see the park badly enough that they made the trip themselves, often driving their own horse-drawn vehicles hundreds of miles to do so. In the years before automobiles invaded the park it was not at all uncommon to see families from all over the region traveling the roads in crude farm wagons—farmers, laborers, and the occasional honeymooners out for the first and probably last such adventure of their lives. "We constantly met the most rustic of vehicles drawn by the roughest of farm animal," wrote one woman visiting Yellowstone in the early 1880s, "filled by the genuine sons and daughters of the soil. It was really strange to see how perfectly this class appreciate the wonders of the place and how glad they are to leave for a while their hard labor for the adventurous, the beautiful, and the sublime. They always carried their outfit, camping every night. I have no doubt that they saw more and enjoyed more than conventional travelers."

The spirit of adventure that set the Peckhams and their six children on the road from their home in Green County, Wisconsin, to see Yellowstone in the spring of 1903 was hardly uncommon. The notion for the trip came to the family when, three years earlier, Mr. Peckham's father made the journey with his wife and "two old maids," and had come back so thrilled with what he saw that the rest of the family decided to make a similar excursion. They covered roughly twenty-five miles a day in two horse-drawn covered wagons and, including time out for visiting relatives along the way, were gone seventeen months. "It was just a sightseeing trip," explained one of the Peckhams' children many years later, when he was eighty-nine, putting off the suggestion of a young newspaper reporter that it was somehow a significant feat.

Another group of three farming families, all of modest means, recorded a six-week trip through the park by wagon in 1880. Besides being thrilled with the scenery, one of the women makes special mention in her journal of the practical applications of the park's thermal features. "The oatmeal we had for breakfast had been cooked slowly all night over a fissure in a small mound, through which rushed hot steam, continually." This isn't to say that such culinary techniques weren't without some risk. "The beans, which were cooking in a flour-sack in a geyser pool, held in place by a pile of small stones, went off with the geyser, and were lost."

And then there's the wonderful story of a thousand-mile trek by spring wagon made by a Mrs. N. E. Corthell and her seven children in 1903, from Laramie, Wyoming. "Now if a timid mother with a wagonload of children (oldest boy not yet sixteen) can take the trip, anybody can, and everybody ought to," she says. It's hard to argue with this woman, especially when she makes the case for how rewarding the experience was for her children. "They played in the Platte, the Sweetwater, the Popo-Agie, the Wind, the Snake, the Yellowstone, Lewis, Firehole, Shoshone, Greybull, Big Horn and Laramie rivers. They have seen their native state as no books can teach it, and came home in the finest health with ravenous appetites.

"Oh, for more Yellowstones to conquer."

Oh, for more Yellowstones indeed.

EIGHT

This morning we eat our eggs and pancakes amidst the dark, glossy wood of the Old Faithful Inn, a staggering medley of timber and rock erected during the winter of 1903–1904 under the direction of designer Robert Reamer. Why Reamer decided to build the inn during the winter is hard to say. One guess is that it was easier to skid the hundreds of tons of timber and foundation stones—the latter were quarried nearly five miles away—over snow than over bare ground. Though few details are known about the actual construction of the Old Faithful, we can assume that things were done in a fashion similar to the way Reamer built the Canyon Hotel seven years later. In that project the kitchen was built first, one reason being so that nails could be heated on the stoves to ward off frostbite in the fingers of the carpenters. Frostbite was such a problem, in fact, that a clinic with a sizable staff of nurses was kept busy throughout the winter months treating it.

No one walks into the lobby of the Old Faithful Inn without being struck by the sheer presence of the place—Gothic form spiked with titanic splashes of the rustic. Whereas most Eastern recreational resorts of the same period were extensions of the English notion of gentility, the designs of the great park hotels like the Old Faithful never strayed too far from the awesome power of nature in the raw. It's true that the Old Faithful Inn was meant to offer a sense of rest in the midst of overpowering wilderness—the dark forests, the strange, vast fields of steaming geysers and mud pots. But far more important was that it offer some degree of expression to the yearnings of an increasingly confined, industrialized middle class, a middle class that was feeling more than a little tightly bound by the conventions of the Victorian era.

The European notion of parks was drastically different from what most Americans deemed appropriate to the boundless spaces of the West. For example, in 1874, Swedish landscape architect Knut Forsberg wrote to the secretary of interior asking that he be given a commission of $132,000 to prepare a collection of maps and models depicting an ultimate vision of what Yellowstone Park should one day be—prototypes of how "nature's own beauty and prosperous vegetation would join with architectural decorations." Among other things, Forsberg's plan included a National Agriculture Institute; a National Natation School (to train swimmers); a National Rowing Club and Racegrounds; a geological museum, botanical gardens, zoological gardens, and a gardeners institute; an extensive health-care facility, including homeopathic clinic and watercure services, and a National Institute for Lake and River Fishing Propagation. When the secretary of interior passed Forsberg's proposal on to U.S. Geological Survey Chief Ferdinand Hayden, one of the founding fathers of Yellowstone, Hayden dismissed it as being utterly excessive. "The park is to be preserved as far as possible in a state of nature with only such improvements as are necessary for the accommodations of tourists and invalids." And thus Forsberg's plan was dead before it hit the ground.

Curiously, architect H. Duane Hampton points out that Forsberg's plan, while certainly inappropriate in a great many respects, might have eliminated the kinds of developmental disasters that occurred in Yellowstone from 1956 to 1966. This ten-year period framed a maniacally ambitious federal program known as Mission 66, designed to upgrade recreational facilities on federal park lands in preparation for increased public use. Unfortunately, when it was all said and done, fully 5 percent of Yellowstone was lost to development, a great deal of it appearing to have had about as much forethought as the Main Street of Dawson in the height of the gold rush. Hampton calls attention to the tacky "shanties" that replaced the beautiful Canyon Hotel, a piece of architecture that was "sacrificed for a hodgepodge of supermarkets, curio shops, ice machines and hutments. [Forsberg's] errant proposals—" Hampton points out, "now gathering dust in the National Archives—might remind present-day dilemma-ridden park administrators not only of what might have been, but of what unfortunately is." Building places like Grant Village, and even going against its own internal recommendations to close out facilities at Fishing Bridge to restore grizzly habitat, have at times made it hard for the Park Service to be taken seriously when it criticizes development on adjacent lands.

I hit the trail alone, once again sporting fifty pounds of gear, bound for the lonely, stream-laden southwest corner of the park. After a routine climb past yet another stretch of burn, it's back into the green of the conifer forest. I've hardly passed the first live spruce tree when I hear a chorus of tiny peeping sounds off to my right. As I turn to look, a female blue grouse comes charging out of the cover, tail spread and neck feathers ruffled, hissing at me with a ferocity that seems way out of proportion to her size. Three times she comes within eighteen inches of my leg before backing off for another run. Only when I've passed ten to fifteen feet from her does she finally turn away and trot back to her brood, which, while remaining completely invisible, can be clearly heard cheering her on in the background.

The trail forks, and though my destination lies down the right branch, I follow the left one for a quick half-mile run to Lone Star Geyser. Lone Star is a good first plum for beginning geyser gawkers. This is the only geyser to be found in the entire area (hence its name), and the forty-foot spout of water it sends skyward every three hours is a show well worth watching. Lone Star is thought to be successor to a large collection of hot springs that were buried thousands of years ago under tons of glacial debris. The calcite cone, which is one of the largest in the park, is beautifully decorated with glistening pink- and silver-colored beads of sinter. (Sinter is merely silica that has precipitated out of the water as it cools.) The reason for Lone Star's impressive cone is that even when the geyser isn't erupting, it pushes generous splashes of water over the lip, leaching out minerals that slowly build the cone higher and higher. This ejected water forms warm rills that run outward across the ground from the base, giving rise to beautiful lines of brightly colored algae. When Frank Bradley of the Hayden Survey party first came upon Lone Star in 1872, he described the cone as having the profile of a mild-featured human face. Either Bradley had a fantastic imagination, or over the past century this particular curiosity has yielded to something decidedly more like the face of an alien.

A Lone Star eruption is definitely a production. It begins with an achingly slow stretch of sloshing and rumbling, gradually increasing in intensity over a two-hour period before finally letting loose with a fifteen-minute-long, forty-foot-high discharge; this is followed by a rather boisterous release of steam. The eruption schedule of Lone Star has stayed remarkably constant over the past hundred years; Old Faithful not withstanding, Lone Star is the most regular of all the Yellowstone geysers.

As you might imagine, many people end up spending a lot of time here just hanging around waiting for an eruption— eating lunch, wandering over for quick looks at the Firehole River, or in some cases, thinking up quips and wisecracks to add to the pages of the logbook found in front of the main viewing area. The last entry before my visit, made by Robert from Denver, reported "a premature ejaculation at 10:51." (Curiously, a number of males selected "premature ejaculation" as the term of choice for describing geyser activity. Either a great many visitors to Lone Star are excitable teenagers, or untimely orgasm is much more of a problem than any of us would have thought. If the latter is true, it seems almost tragic that someone would walk four long, hot miles through grizzly country only to have Mother Nature remind him of an embarrassing sexual problem.) Most comments are decidedly less Freudian, though—mostly just enthusiastic endorsements for how beautiful Lone Star really is: "Two trips back here today to see the show. Well worth it"; "One of the best in the park"; "The rainbow that forms in the steam is out of this world!"; and finally "Major blowout, dude!"

I am alone until just before the eruption occurs, at which point two clinicians from the Lake infirmary arrive. We chat for a while, and when I happen to ask them if they see many wildlife-related injuries, both of them roll their eyes back and shake their heads. "In the six weeks we've been here, we've had four buffalo gorings," the man explains. "Most of the people knew they were gambling—they come in feeling pretty sheepish about the whole thing. But last week we got a woman who was chasing a cow and calf around trying to get in close for the perfect picture, when she got hooked in the side with a horn. Now she says that the Park Service should shoot the animal and pay all her medical bills." Short of putting shock collars on the tourists, it's hard to imagine how park managers could give any more warnings about bison danger than they already do.

Retracing my route back to the Howard Eaton Trail, I move south again, crossing the Firehole River at four miles, and passing fine spatters of sticky geraniums, harebells, paintbrush, lupine, shrubby cinquefoil, and mountain dandelion along the way. The name "Firehole" may have been given to this river in 1850 by no less than Jim Bridger, the consummate liar and imagineer, though a valley west of here near Hebgen Lake (or "hole," as trappers liked to call mountain valleys), is thought to have carried the same name years earlier. True to his reputation, Bridger informed Captain W. F. Raynolds that the reason for the stream's warm temperature was that it "flowed so fast down the side of the hill that the friction of the water against the rocks heated the rocks."

In comparison to some of Bridger's other tales about the Yellowstone country, this one seems almost believable. There was his trip to the petrified forest, which was thick with flowers, deer, and elk all perfectly preserved in stone, not to mention petrified birds sitting in petrified trees singing petrified songs. While passing near the Lamar Valley one day, Bridger's horse walked right off the edge of a precipice near Specimen Ridge, but didn't fall to the ground. Confused at first, Bridger finally attributed it to—what else?—petrified gravity. And then there was the story about one of Bridger's favorite camping spots. It was opposite a large, flat-faced mountain so far away that it took an echo six hours to return. Using this fact to his advantage, just before turning in at night Bridger would let out a cry of "time to get up!" and sure enough, at dawn the next morning that wake-up call would come floating back.

A short distance past the Firehole I enter an open corridor filled with a clamor of burps and bubbles rising from a cluster of football-sized holes in the ground. If hell really is down there, as a few people during the nineteenth century seemed to believe, then somebody seems to have dumped bicarbonate into Lucifer's swimming pool. At one point early into this stretch of trail, just when I'm in the middle of some sweet reverie, a hole right next to the trail vents with a sudden rush, scaring me half out of my pack straps.

For some time there was strong opinion that all Native Americans strictly avoided Yellowstone's thermal areas, fearing them to be the home of evil spirits. Before General Sherman visited the park in 1877, he wrote a letter to a concerned Secretary of War, saying that he saw no danger to his trip since Indians would steer clear of a place that was "to their superstitious minds associated with hell by reason of its geysers and hot-springs."

And yet the archaeological record shows otherwise. Occupational sites have been discovered in the thermal areas at Norris Basin, Gibbon Basin, and at Sulphur Mountain, as well as along the Yellowstone River, the Firehole River, the Thumb on Yellowstone Lake, and even near Mammoth and Old Faithful. What's more, while some oral histories from various tribes do include stories about avoiding the geysers altogether, others talk of men bathing in the pools. True, some tribes with limited experience in the region, like the Blackfeet, the plains Shoshone, and the Kalispell, probably were frightened by the geysers, and avoided them if possible. But others, most notably the Sheepeaters, the Bannock, and perhaps the Crow and even the Nez Perce, may have had little fear of them at all.

Of those tribes who did steer clear of the thermal areas, it was likely much less a matter of their thinking them filled with evil spirits, than that these features simply had powers with which they had no relationship. To this day there are traditional Native Americans who still offer gifts when traveling through unfamiliar regions, an act that's in large part based on a concern that they might mistakenly cause offense because they don't know the ways of that particular place. Several stories from the historical record suggest that Native Americans bathed in the hot pools to try to develop an alliance with the powers there, and thus perhaps procure whatever medicine those powers had to offer.

Clearly, infatuation with hell and evil is much more a trait of white visitors and explorers than of Native Americans. And, given the Christian preoccupation with wickedness, it's easy to see how one might interpret the offering of gifts to a geyser basin as an attempt to please an angry, fearsome god. Indeed, this tendency to project a European view of the cosmos on other cultures is found in much of our so-called "Indian lore." A good example is a 1933 story called "the fable of the geysers," which says the Indians believed that evil spirits under the geyser basins threw hot water on the spouts so that animals couldn't drink there. And then there is Father DeSmet's 1850 account of how Indians thought geysers were the abode of warring underground spirits who were "continually at the anvil forging their weapons." Never mind that at that time the Indians had no knowledge of blacksmithing.

It was not the Indians, after all, who called thermal features by names like Devil's Cauldron, Demon's Cave, and Dante's Inferno. Making a trip through Yellowstone in 1872, Lord

William Blackmore talked of a particular series of thermal springs as being "horrible and appalling." It was easy to believe, he claimed, "that you have at length come to the entrance to the infernal regions. I have never seen anything so thoroughly diabolical in my life." Nathaniel Langford talked of a thermal area south of Mount Washburn in even more disagreeable terms: "The spring lying to the east, more diabolical in appearance, [was] filled with a brownish substance of the consistence of thin mucilage, emitting fumes of villainous odor. It suggested the name, which we gave, of Hell Broth Springs. This was a most perfect realization of Shakespeare's image in Macbeth—and I fancied the 'black and midnight hags' concocting a charm around this horrible cauldron." (Fortunately, not all early visitors were so infatuated with the notion of Hades hiding beneath the surface of Yellowstone. While trapper Joe Meek was definitely taken aback by Yellowstone's whistling steam vents and ominous-looking plugs of brimstone, in the end he likened the place not to hell, but to "Pittsburgh on a winter morning.")

On the plus side, giving descriptive names to thermal features, whether references to hell or to heaven, is much more satisfying than using personal names. For this we can thank the Washburn party, as well as explorers like F. V. Hayden, who decided early on that names of people would not be applied to any hot spring, geyser, mud pot, or steam vent. And, with less than a handful of exceptions, that has always been the case. Hayden did a great job of summing up his attitude in a letter he wrote to Arnold Hague in 1885. What could be more absurd, he asks, than Arthur Geyser?

There's something different about the stretch of trail beyond the crossing of the Firehole River. Today the wildness here seems somehow deeper, a "far north" mosaic of tightly woven meadows framed by long reaches of spruce and fir, the timber murky and somber in even the brightest sunlight. Ten feet beyond the edge of the meadows is the kind of dark, strange woodland that poet Edward Thomas must have had in mind when he wrote "Lights Out":

I have come to the borders of sleep,
The unfathomable deep
Forest where all must lose
Their way, however straight,
Or winding, soon or late;
They cannot choose.

While all forests hold for me the promise of adventure, on rare occasions they can also bring on an irrational sense of danger. It would be in just this type of place that my conception of grizzly country might suddenly slide from a source of awe into something far more uncertain and foreboding. In the world's great myths, when a person is swallowed into the unknown—as Jonah was by the whale, and as virtually all the Greek gods were by Kronos—it is seen as a metaphor for entering a state of rebirth, a return to earthly paradise. The reason that such entry points are usually guarded—by dragons, the teeth of a whale, or, on many of the world's great temples, by fierce-looking gargoyles—is not to keep everyone out, but to remind us that this netherworld is reserved for only those willing to fully embrace the inner reaches of their being. When my thoughts of being in grizzly country suddenly turn from fascination to horror, not in the face of any real threat but of a purely imagined one, I can't help but wonder if it's because for the time being I've lost the ability to reconcile my inner landscapes with the outer ones.

Such feelings usually come on with no warning. One minute I'm thrilled to be here, and the next my pace has quickened and my eyes are scanning the woods in all directions for hints of movement. Fortunately these sensations aren't all that common, and they usually pass in a few minutes. But within this small window of apprehension I can well appreciate how the notion of being separate from the land is a seed that can grow into the need to subdue it at any cost. What would the world be like, I wonder, if our religions and philosophies had specialized in teaching us how to walk through the shadows of the unknown, instead of merely handing us plans for erecting forts along the outer edges?

Fifty yards to the right a branch breaks off with a loud crack. More than likely it's an elk, but I waste no time loosening my pack belt and scanning the fringe of the forest for a good climbing tree. If the guardian of the inner worlds is coming wrapped in a bear suit, then I'm determined to make my first acquaintance from atop a stout spruce branch, a good twelve feet off the ground.

Soon the path leaves the meadow and begins climbing through the timber toward Grant's Pass, along the low, rolling ridge tops of the Continental Divide—a route once intended to be a railroad line running south through the park to Jackson Hole. The mosquitoes are growing worse by the minute, and by the time I reach the base of Grant's Pass, they have become intolerable. Though I'm well coated in bug dope, more than a few manage to wing their way in for a bite, while dozens of others hover about my ears, whining at that certain pitch that drives humans crazy. When Lord William Blackmore visited Yellowstone from England in the summer of 1872, he found the mosquitoes to be one of the great drawbacks of the park. In fact, in his diary he spends more time talking about being repulsed by bugs than by his encounter with Rocky Mountain Phil Gardner (not to be confused with Johnson Gardner), an incredibly crude trapper who, at least once on finding himself hungry in the backcountry, was rumored to have shot his Indian guide and eaten him on the spot.

The forest remains thick and green along the Continental Divide, and the roll of the terrain is so slight that I can get very little sense of what lies beyond. Beneath the trees is a thick blanket of whortleberry, while the edges of the path are strewn with spring beauties and one-eyed daisies. The wind is running heavy with the smell of pine. My campsite for tonight is pleasant enough, but the mosquitoes are so bad that I use up much of the remaining daylight lying in the tent, making notes and consulting my field guides. When do I finally dash out to cook dinner, there isn't a single move I can make— lighting the stove, opening a tea bag, pouring water—that isn't followed by a series of swats.

As I'm choking down my last spoonful of rice in the dark, I hear voices coming up the trail—odd, considering that these are reserved, one-party camps, and the next nearest site is several miles away. Soon a young woman approaches with five teenagers following close behind, all of them clearly exhausted. "Hello!" she calls, obviously surprised to see my tent. "Uhh . . . I think this is our camp." Her name is Sally. She's about twenty-two, lean and muscular with a brown, weathered face and blonde hair that the sun has washed to the color of straw. Her hands, small but strong, are dappled with smudges of pine pitch. Sally works as a tour leader, taking young adults from all over the country on backpacking trips through the northern Rockies. The kids who are with her now make up the advanced group, which is a very good thing, because after having gotten lost early in the day, they have walked twenty-six miles to reach this place, fighting bugs and finally darkness, only to find it occupied by me.

We check our permit stubs, and sure enough, the Park Service has booked us all into the same tiny unit. "We're getting used to it," Sally says offhandedly. "Last night they double-booked us too. There were fifteen of us, and we busted in on a father who'd waited two years to have some quiet time with his son." All of us make the best of it, which as far as I'm concerned isn't hard to do. The kids are spirited and full of fun, even after their twenty-six-mile ordeal. In fact, after three days on the trail, they seem thoroughly intoxicated—not only with what they've seen and done, but with the camaraderie that's grown between them, a camaraderie that's particularly intriguing in that it seems to have few gender boundaries. How great, I think as I listen to them tossing jests back and forth, it would have been for the guys of my generation to have shared such experiences with young women. To go out on adventures like this, to have walked into the mountains together under heavy packs and been collectively astonished—well, it seems like a reasonable stepping-stone along the path to a more equitable culture.

The next morning I'm up early, and as I pack up my gear

I can hear moans floating over from the other tents, the sound of aching muscles starting to rebel. Just as I start to leave camp the first of the young hikers stumbles out from under the rain fly, blinking hard, checking his arms for the first signs of mosquitoes. "Morning," I offer. "How'd you sleep?"

"Sleeping was easy," he says. "This is the hard part." I assure him again that the trip to Shoshone Lake will seem like a walk in the mall compared to what he went through yesterday, but behind his thin smile I sense major doubts, as if he's heard such assurances before. We wish each other well, and I set off westward, the cool morning air raising goose-bumps on the calves of my legs.

The first three miles of trail is through a fine reach of meadow, the near horizon dominated by the abrupt shoulders of Douglas Knob. Joe Douglas, who in 1921 wore the twin titles of assistant chief ranger and chief buffalo keeper for Yellowstone National Park, was a ranger's ranger—that sterling blend of good humor and sheer, gritty ability that tended to spawn the best in local ranger lore. In 1927, Douglas, who was in his fifties at the time, was out on winter patrol in thirty-below-zero weather, attempting a crossing of an icebound Yellowstone Lake at West Thumb. Warm springs rise adjacent to and slightly out from the south shore of the lake, and Douglas had the great misfortune to find one. Before he knew what happened he was up to his neck in lake water; had he not been able to grab the skis he'd been carrying on his shoulder at the time, more than likely he would have submerged completely. Given this troubling turn of events, the most obvious choice would have been to make a hasty two-mile retreat back to West Thumb Station. But no, not Douglas. He stripped naked, wrung what water had not already turned to ice from his clothes, put them back on, and hiked fifteen miles to the other side of the lake. The next day, he did twenty more. When a park employee asked the obvious question—why he hadn't returned to West Thumb—Douglas got a sheepish look on his face. "They'd have kidded me to death," was all he said.

A short walk past Douglas Knob I reach the first of several

streams that form the Bechler River. This is entryway into one of the more remote corners of Yellowstone, a place of countless icy water runs pouring off the high plateaus, bound for the shimmering meadowlands to the southwest. Frank Bradley, the same Bradley who made the first official record of Lone Star Geyser, named this river for Gustavus R. Bechler, a rather cantankerous map maker who accompanied the great surveyor Ferdinand Hayden on his explorations of Yellowstone in 1872. Little is known about Bechler, and one can almost imagine that Bradley chose the name because he couldn't think of anyone else. In truth it would have made much more sense had this river been named for Osborne Russell, who had been poking around the main Bechler and its various tributaries looking for beaver thirty-four years earlier. It was along this river that Russell discovered one of the most beautiful waterfalls he'd ever seen. And by that time, four years after he'd first joined Nathaniel Wyeth's Rocky Mountain expedition in 1834, you can bet that Osborne Russell had seen some beautiful waterfalls.

Walking into the Bechler drainage on a warm summer day is quite unlike any other experience in Yellowstone. The forests are draped like tattered green shawls across the rugged headlands, below which are scattered patches of earth completely covered with pink and birchleaf spirea, wild rose, twinberry, raspberry, monkeyflower, thimbleberry, bluebells, columbine, and anemone. The further down the path I go, the more dramatic the scene becomes, the canyon broadening, the growling rapids cutting faster and deeper as the river runs hard for the grassy flats below.

There is water everywhere: booming torrents like fifty-five-foot-high Twister Falls, the frothy curtains of Ragged Falls, and countless veils of spring water pouring off the lips of the Madison and Pitchstone plateaus. At the base of the larger falls are deep, cobalt-colored plunge pools, paradise for more than a few trout, who grow large here lurking in the shadows, dining on mayflies and stoneflies. At camp tonight the first thing I do is take an evening plunge in the frigid water. This is a daily ritual for me, driven not just by the desire to wash away the layers of sweat and bug spray, but by the power of the stream or river to shake me out of whatever fog or stupor that's built up during the afternoon. My muscles tighten and my teeth clench, and I run out naked onto the bank whooping like a madman, crying yes! to the whole big blast of the universe. After having practiced this for several years, I'm quite sure that you don't jump into icy streams and lakes because you're crazy. You do it because you want to get that way.

At the point the Bechler finally reaches the meadows at the mouth of the canyon, nine miles and two thousand feet below its wild, urgent beginnings, it is a different river entirely—a confident but placid twist of water that no longer talks in shouts, but in whispers. Great blankets of grass spread southward from the banks as far as the eye can see, backed on the horizon by the ragged, rocky snouts of the Tetons. Across the river the trail continues west to distance itself from all those incessant meanderings, not turning south until it can make a long, uninterrupted run down the valley. Even though following the banks would add countless miles to the trip, there is a strong part of me that would love to do just that. This is a stretch of river that the gods obviously built for amblers. Rounding corners is like opening presents, the bends holding ducks or beaver, or sometimes, only silent, glistening sheets of mountain water.

Walking through this incredible sprawl of grass and sky and river and mountain, elk and moose drifting in and out of the ragged edges of the forest, it's inconceivable to me that for years there was a powerful movement to dam much of this region to store water for farmers in Idaho. By 1920 proposals by both Idaho and Montana to build dams in Yellowstone—one in the Bechler River country and another on the Yellowstone River just below the lake—had gained enough support that both the secretary of interior and the director of the Park Service felt obliged to denounce the plans in their annual reports. The comments of Park Service Director Stephen Mather are as appropriate today as they were seventy-five years ago: "Are we to relinquish even one square mile of the choicest exhibits of our great national recreational areas without considering their untold value as the breathing spaces for the countless generations yet to come? Cannot we preserve a few of our magnificent lakes, a few of the priceless waterfalls, without encountering the grasping, calloused hand of commercialism extended to deprive our children of their heritage?"

Strange as it may seem, one of the problems during the early struggle to dam the Bechler was that the Park Service had little firsthand knowledge of the area; in fact, not a single superintendent had visited the southwestern corner of the park for at least twenty-six years. Thus it was nearly impossible for park officials to refute the claims of the reservoir company that the area affected by the impoundment was little more than a swamp, and that there was absolutely nothing here in the way of unusual scenery or other interesting features. "The entire area," said one report, "contains only ordinary western mountain landscape scenes. When this reservoir is constructed this swamp will be converted into a beautiful mountain lake." Such statements were given full credibility by no less than the director of the U.S. Reclamation Service, who informed Congress that these magnificent lands were "unsightly," and that reservoirs would be "a distinct improvement in the appearance of the region."

So strong was the opposition from the Park Service, Bureau of Biological Survey, various politicians, and ultimately the public at large, that the measure eventually died in the House of Representatives. Six years later, it was back. This time dam proponents pushed to have nearly thirteen thousand acres in the southwestern corner of the park deleted and turned over to the Forest Service, which was much more accommodating to private development projects. Congressman Addison T. Smith, who six years earlier spoke of building a reservoir in the park with the gusto of a preacher at a tent revival, claimed he was a changed man. "Now it is proposed," he informed Congress, "to eliminate this section from the park, and not conflict with the policy, with which I thoroughly agree, to prevent any economic development inside the lines of the park." In exchange, the park would gain 64,000 acres of nearby national forest.

Among those eager and able to do battle in this particular round of water wars was none other than Yellowstone Superintendent Horace Albright. Albright blasted claims that the Cascade Corner was a place without scenic value, first by describing its beauties, and secondly, by pointing out that the minds of engineers "run not to scenery, but to dams." To prove this contention, Albright offered a case in point. "We have arguments that we should run telephone lines through the park to the geysers, and that it would not spoil the scenery. The engineers say that people should be glad to see a fine telephone line so as to see how well you are protected by the works of man." The bottom line, Albright assured Congress, was that such a transfer could not be done without setting a precedent that might mean the beginning of the end of the national parks.

Proponents of the Bechler project continually refuted the notion that their reservoirs would set a precedent. Yet in truth they were licking their lips over other projects in the park even before the Bechler plan had come to a vote. In a letter written in 1920 to the secretary of agriculture, Idaho Commissioner of Reclamation Swendson shows the real depth of his appetite for irrigation water: "Of course if favorable action is taken [on the Bechler], a precedent will have been established which later should result in use of Yellowstone Lake . . . "

While today rivers like the Bechler seem safe from exploitation within Yellowstone Park, the same can hardly be said for those outside park boundaries. When the Idaho Water Resources Board released a draft plan for state water development recently, conservationists were shocked. Nearly two dozen possible hydroelectric projects and a similar number of reservoirs were listed, including four hydroelectric generation stations on the beautiful Falls River, a seventeen-mile-long reservoir on the Teton River that would inundate twenty-five square miles of valuable wetlands, and a hydroelectric plant on the Henry's Fork, at magnificent Mesa Falls.

•

As the day winds on, I realize that I've probably never had a more satisfying meadow walk than this one. The spaces are vast almost beyond comprehension, and at times the distant horizon approaches so slowly that it seems I'm on some kind of treadmill—hairgrass and wheatgrass, vetches and larkspur blooms rolling slowly underfoot, but the rugged mountains in the distance merely projections against a wash of sky. Were it not for an occasional stream crossing, it would be hard to believe that I was making any mileage at all. Moose rise from the banks of the river, looking at me with that peculiar, yet rather noble goggle that only moose can seem to muster. Overhead the sky is pinned with the silhouettes of soaring hawks and ravens, the latter throwing their gritty calls at whatever other birds they happen to find perched in the conifers nearby. By two o'clock I'm drunk on the place, knowing that no matter what crud or crises may plague me in the 250 miles of trail that yet remain, I will always have this perfect summer afternoon to retreat into. Little do I know that the fun is just beginning—that before darkness rolls across the Bechler, I will have had one of the most enjoyable nature experiences of my life.

It begins as soon as I walk into my riverside camp, when a fine young cow moose ambles out of the forest on the other side of the river, crosses over, and begins a casual feast of willow and pondweed. There she will stay for a good hour before swaggering off, returning twice more before dark. When she finally leaves the first time I pitch my tent beside a patch of bedstraw, take a good long swim, and then find a comfortable perch in the shade of a lodgepole. There are great puffs of cumulus clouds drifting across the sky. Beneath me, along five gentle bends of the river, countless rings spread across the surface of the water as trout rise to feed on mosquitoes. Tree swallows zig and zag through the air, nabbing insects on the wing, while butterflies flutter among the ivory-colored umbels of yampa and yarrow. In the meadows to the west I can hear the chortle of sandhill cranes.

Just as I'm about to nod off from terminal bliss, a western

tanager lights in the tree above my head, a bright flash of tropical color flitting from branch to branch in a thorough search for insects. It's fortunate that this tanager has come to rescue me from sleep, because almost from this moment on the river corridor becomes the stage for what seems like the Mardi Gras of animal parades. First a female merganser drifts past with her brood of young chicks; were they to sense danger from me, the entire family could disappear beneath the water in the blink of an eye. Mergansers are among the best underwater swimmers anywhere (the young can dive as soon as they hit the water), and adults routinely chase and capture the swiftest of fish with ease. A hundred yards behind the mergansers, a family of mallards, led by one of the most steadfast, indomitable mothers in all the bird world, begins a similar downstream trek through the green ribbons of aquatic grass. The act ends with a beautiful osprey winging her way up the river corridor looking for fish, the air making sounds like whispers as it rushes beneath her wings.

When I finally get up to fix dinner, the moose returns, and we eat more or less together—she nabbing mouthfuls of willow and sedge, and me going after a pot of rice. We don't say much to one another, but do exchange an occasional stare across the thirty or so yards that separate us. In truth she's an excellent dinner companion, and I hope she finds me at least a pleasant curiosity. As I finish cleaning up the dishes and hang the food, the moose ambles away once again, and five minutes later an entire family of beaver comes swimming up the river against the far bank. They continue a hundred yards past me, and then leave the bank to frolic in the middle of the current. One of the adults slaps its tail several times with a loud crack, water splashing all about him, but he doesn't seem to mean it as any kind of warning; he and the rest of the beaver continue to chase each other as if danger were days away. After a time they leave, continuing upstream, and not fifteen minutes later, much to my utter delight, comes a lone adult otter, pausing in front of the camp long enough to give me a thorough going over. More than likely this is a male who, having already sired young, has left mom with the task of teaching the kids how to swim and catch food, to rejoin them sometime in September. Otters are sleek, graceful animals, capable of swimming underwater at speeds of up to six miles per hour. They're also notorious characters, and will chase each other, slide down mud and snow banks, and even toss sticks around while floating in the water. When this fellow reaches a point slightly upstream from where I sit, he suddenly dives, and comes up twenty seconds later with a cutthroat trout. He then rolls over on his back and eats it off his stomach, drifting slowly back downstream, glancing over at me every so often, as if showing me a chapter of the good life according to otters. A duck whistles by overhead, and then it is quiet once again.

By this time I am thoroughly entranced, feeling as if I've fallen through some kind of cosmic crack and ended up, if not in Wonderland, then at least in an old Disney movie. It is as close as I will probably ever get to the aboriginal concept of dream time. My tape recorder is on and I'm whispering the details of every creature's passing, and six months later I will still be smiling when I listen to the thrill in my voice as I describe how each event unfolds. And more visitors: Swimming on the far side of the river, nibbling on sedges and the bulbs of various aquatic plants, is a family of muskrats. After they're weaned, young muskrats build their own summer residences and then stay there until fall (after which Mom and Dad boot them from the territory), so this must be the second litter of the season.

While many people tend to think of the muskrat as a fairly ordinary animal, in Blackfeet legend he is said to have done nothing less than help turn the earth into an inhabitable place for land-dwelling creatures. Long ago there was a lone old man living on earth, and one fateful spring there came a great flood. To escape the rising water the man climbed up into the hills, but still it rose, higher and higher, until at last the only refuge to be found was on top of a tall mountain, where he was joined by four animals: beaver, otter, duck, and muskrat.

Though he was a very powerful old man, try as he might he couldn't get the waters to recede. Frustrated, he turned to the animals, telling them that in order for him to create dry land, he had to have a dab of mud—the smallest amount would do. He told the beaver to see if he could find some. The beaver agreed to try, and down he went into the depths of the sea.

Sadly, after a long time of waiting, the old man spied the beaver's lifeless body floating on the surface of the water. The otter agreed to go next, but, just like the beaver, she too died trying. When the duck's turn came, she managed to go surprisingly deep, but she came back to the surface unconscious, with no mud in her bill to offer the old man. And then it was time for the muskrat. He was gone for a long, long while, and the old man thought him surely dead. But finally he appeared again, and though he too was unconscious, he held on the pads of his front paws a tiny dab of the precious mud. The old man took the mud, placed it in the palm of his hand, and blew on it, whereupon it grew bigger and bigger, until it had grown into all the land we see today. And when the land was restored, the old man made the plants, and all the living things.

There are very few clouds in the western sky. The sun goes down easy, gently dousing the coral light that lays unruffled on the river, and then slowly pulling shadows up the trunks and branches of the fir and pines. I do not often build a fire in summer, but tonight I do. Tonight is different, and I feel like being surrounded by the old symbols of life on the ground—the smell of smoke, the warmth and color of the flames. In the very last of the light I try to write a few notes, but it's nearly impossible to see what I'm doing. And besides, right now I'm not up to interpretations. It seems better just to lay a few more sticks on the fire. And dream.

Over the years I've been fortunate enough to see some dazzling wildlife displays, from fish eagles hunting on the Zambezi River to great flocks of flamingos dropping onto the still waters of Africa's Ngorongoro Crater at sunset. But I have enjoyed none of it any more than I enjoyed this magic evening on the Bechler. It feels good to touch wild things within the borders of my homeland, to stare across the water into the eyes of my neighbors the moose and the otter. Even if I were to never set foot in this land again I'd rest easier knowing that these animals were here, much the way I can take solace from the thought of composers out there creating new music, whether or not that music ever falls on my ears. I am clearly a different person during my exchanges with the creatures of the wilds. And I sense whatever it is that rises to consciousness during those times, is something that's been hidden in the shadows for much too long.

Instead of taking the main route south out of the park past the Bechler Ranger Station, I veer off to the southeast, making my way to Flagg Ranch Road along a series of little-used paths, wandering back and forth through an easy mix of burn and meadows and green trees. The streams, most notably Mountain Ash Creek and Falls River, are big and wide here, and roll as clear as sheets of crystal in the mountain sun. In the roughly nine miles of my trek to the road, I do not see another person; indeed, the land seems to grow wilder and more remote with every step, and the trails—especially over the last four miles—deteriorate slowly but surely, until they are little more than deer paths.

A short distance after turning east onto the Boundary Trail I reach Calf Creek, which at this point is a twenty-foot-wide reach of slack water with no bridge, just a few old planks and weathered logs strewn about the banks. At most streams this time of year I'd simply switch my hiking boots for river sandals and trudge across. But there are yellow pond lilies growing throughout this channel, and pond lilies are an indication of deep water; savvy fly fishermen consider these plants a warning not to approach an area, since more than likely the water will be above the tops of their chest waders. I search up and down the broad valley for alternatives, but there are none. Downstream it is more of the same; upstream to the south conditions are even worse, as the channel bleeds into a full-blown swamp.

Stripped of all but shorts and water sandals, I ease off the bank into the murky water, trying to determine how bad the situation really is. Immediately my feet sink into fifteen inches of dark, rich slime—a splendid nutrient milkshake for billions of organisms, but for walkers a slimy, gooey morass that sucks at your feet and smells like last week's omelet. By the time I get a yard off the bank the stream has deepened, leaving me almost neck deep in brown water. Fortunately, by complete accident my foot happens to kick an old bridge support laying on the bottom; by walking carefully, as if on a balance beam, I at least have a solid surface that keeps me from sinking past my neck. But while the log is long enough to take me almost all the way across, there is no way I can walk it holding a fifty-pound pack above my head.

Returning to the bank, I scour the willow thickets and find two old bridge planks, which I lash together with nylon rope to form the simplest, crudest of rafts onto which I can lay my pack. By carefully walking on the old log lying in the muck and pushing my pack along ahead of me, I eventually—ever so slowly, it seems—make it to the other side. As I'm drying off and changing back into my boots, I happen to notice a small faded sign atop a tilted, weathered post along the trail.

WARNING—Bridge Unsafe and Closed to Stock Use
Hikers Use at Your Own Risk

From here nearly to Flagg Ranch Road the trail has had almost no use. At one point it disappears completely in a vast corridor of seven-foot-tall willow thickets, leaving me to wander around like a mouse in a maze. Further east in the Calf Creek drainage the path fades again, this time into thick carpets of bluebell, campion, paintbrush, huckleberry, and sticky geranium; when it is visible, it's often blocked by toppled spruce logs. As the trail leaves the lowlands it does so in a fairly big way, climbing seven hundred feet in just over half a mile. The final stretch winds along a small, precipitous canyon, the edge of which is strewn with beautiful slabs and loaves of 350-million-year-old limestone and dolomite, much of it carved by ice, wind, and water into the most engaging shapes imaginable. The inaccessible lower walls of the canyon receive regular mistings from Calf Creek, and, being generally out of reach of the sun's hot fingers, sport thick, emerald-green gardens of moss and semiaquatic plants. Looking down from the edge, it seems like a last blast of fantasy, an exclamation point to my last day in Yellowstone National Park.

NINE

Walking out of Yellowstone's pristine Cascade Corner into the Targhee National Forest is like heading out the door after an afternoon at the Louvre, only to find yourself standing in a junkyard. It would be hard to find a more dramatic example of how historically this region has been treated not as a single ecosystem, managed according to the ebb and flow of the various natural processes, but as a hodgepodge of unconnected zones of use and abuse. Massive clear-cuts have occurred all the way up to the very border of Yellowstone; seen from the air, the park boundary is as unwavering as if it had been drawn by a straightedge—lodgepole forest lying east of the line in Yellowstone Park, and hot, shadeless swells of grass and dozer ruts to the west, on the Targhee.

As I stumble around trying to find the Bitch Creek Trail (now also destroyed by clear-cuts), the area looks more ravaged than I could have imagined. This is no longer a forest but a commodity site, a slice of land with about as much complexity and intrigue as a stadium parking lot. These scars, which stretch as far as the eye can see, are the scars that come not from the mere harvesting of resources but from a tough, grinding campaign more akin to corporate farming than to prudent, conscientious forestry. More than five years after replanting, the land looks miserable. Only a few one- to three-foot-tall seedlings have survived, and those are often thirty or forty yards from their nearest neighbor. True, with time the lodgepole forest will return here, thanks to the fact that lodgepole seedlings are incredibly adept at reclaiming disturbed areas. But the former Douglas fir stands just to the west, also wiped clean, will not fare so well, since the seedlings of that species cannot survive without the cover of older trees. From the look of reclamation efforts there, someone might as well have driven through the cuts in a pickup truck, tossing pine cones out the window.

Until recently, of all the timber cut in the seven national forests of the Yellowstone ecosystem, more than half came from this one. In 1960 the Targhee opened a sale of 318 million board feet—the largest ever offered in the continental United States—and for a time firewood cuts alone were being permitted at the rate of 105 million board feet per year. Although by 1980 the cut had declined significantly, the annual harvest during the rest of the decade was nearly four times the amount harvested on the adjacent Gallatin National Forest.

One would assume that with this many trees being sold the forest would have been raking in a significant income. Not so. While for years the Targhee had the highest annual cut in the region, at the same time it lost more money on its timber program than any other forest. (In 1990, the Forest Service admitted that more than half of the country's 122 national forests lost money on their timber programs, though Congressional economists placed the number closer to 85 percent. Researchers placed total losses to the U.S. Treasury from these below-cost timber sales at over 200 million dollars annually; over the last decade, the figure may rest somewhere between 2 and 5 billion dollars.)

In all fairness, a significant amount of the annual cut on the Targhee through the last half of the 1970s—roughly 80 million to 100 million board feet per year—was part of a massive salvage of lodgepoles killed by pine bark beetles, an insect that tends to prey on trees more than eighty years old. Up until that time the forest had spent 10 million dollars trying to control beetle populations through a fumigation program. Unfortunately, later studies showed that the poisons being used, most especially lindane, tended to kill the insects that preyed on bark beetles far more often than it killed the beetles themselves.

While few question the appropriateness of harvesting beetle kill, the Targhee acted as if it were having a going-out-of-business sale. Fallen trees create important habitat for small mammals, as well as various kinds of invertebrates. Equally important, standing beetle kill provides an important measure of cover for large game like elk and grizzly bears. Biologists blame the severe decline in the quality of elk herds in this area not on the spread of the pine bark beetle, but on the massive cuts that have laced much of the region with a vast network of roads and large, open tracts of land, both of which elk tend to avoid. To give an idea of what's really happening here, prior to the start of massive cutting programs the elk hunting season on the Targhee was forty-four days long, and both cows and bulls could be taken. By 1990, even though the total number of hunters was similar, the general season was just five days long, and hunters could take only bulls. Researchers on the Island Park district soon discovered that because logging roads had so dramatically increased accessibility to the animals, the majority of bulls were no longer living beyond the first hunting season. By the fall of 1991, the herd was so depleted that hunters were allowed to take nothing but yearlings, or "spike" bulls.

Thirty years ago, had you taken a summer stroll through this part of the Targhee you would have stood a fairly good chance of seeing elk. Today such sightings are rare. The only large groups that frequent the area at all are migratory herds coming out of Yellowstone, bound for winter range at Sand Creek. Because of the danger posed by roads and clear-cuts, these animals pass through with great haste, making a trip that used to take them close to thirty days in barely two. According to the Idaho Fish and Game Department, this profound change in migratory behavior, combined with the severe loss of resident animals, has reduced hunter opportunity by 75 percent—hardly good news to a region that traditionally raked in more than 4 million dollars annually from deer and elk hunting on this forest alone. Ironically, logging and outfitting were long considered among the most important forest-related jobs in this region; years of overharvesting, however, has severely crippled both.

Grizzlies fare no better under massive cutting programs than do elk. In the late 1980s a sale was proposed for the Island Park District of the Targhee National Forest (a sale some say was expressly designed to stimulate the region's flagging timber industry) that would have removed the last strips of forest dividing previous timber sales on the Moose Creek Plateau near the border of Yellowstone. Despite the fact that two grizzly dens were found within a mile of the proposed sale, the forest failed to acknowledge any potential harm to the bears. In another proposed sale very near to where I now stand in Situation One grizzly habitat (lands considered critical to grizzly survival), the Targhee not only claimed "no significant impact," but at one time actually suggested that the cut would improve grizzly bear habitat, despite a significant amount of research indicating that clear-cutting and road building does just the opposite.

For all of Targhee's sordid past, today this forest has managers on the ground who seem to be striving for positive change. More selective cutting programs (as opposed to clearcutting) are scheduled to be in place by 1993, and there is a push to significantly reduce the size of clear-cuts. In 1990 the annual harvest had already dropped to 20 million board feet, and further reductions are planned.

Ironically, as the foresters themselves finally begin to manage these lands more in line with legal mandates, the region's politicians stand by, ready to punish anyone who threatens to diminish the cut. Incensed by plans to reduce harvesting on the Targhee, in May of 1991 Republican Senator Larry Craig wrote to Forest Service Chief Dale Robertson, informing him of "serious management problems that must be addressed." (Craig, incidentally, is the same senator who in 1986 thought it would be nice to punch a paved road through Idaho's magnificent River of No Return Wilderness to increase accessibility.) Similar tactics have been used against Ernie Nunn, supervisor of Montana's Helena National Forest, who angered politicians and industry groups by setting sound, no-nonsense standards for mining in the Elkhorn Mountains. Nunn tried to strike a more even balance between logging, mining, and recreation here, though with the Forest Service funding 100 percent of its timber programs and only 50 percent of both wildlife and recreation, that was hardly easy. Not long ago, some say at the urgings of Montana politicians, the agency forced Nunn into reassignment.

Also under the corporate/political gun was John Mumma, the first biologist ever to land the position of regional forester in the Northern Rockies, and some say one of better land managers in the entire system. Tom Kovalicky, retired supervisor of Idaho's Nez Perce Forest, once wrote in a memo to other federal foresters that John Mumma "is the only regional forester in recent times who is fighting for resource balance." When several Western Republican senators complained to Department of Agriculture Secretary Edward Madigan that Mumma wasn't cutting enough trees, Madigan suddenly decided that it was time for Mumma to start pushing pencils at a desk in Washington, D.C. No options. No discussion. Instead, Mumma resigned. "I find it strange," Mumma said at Congressional hearings, "that I am reassigned for meeting approximately 85 percent of my timber target, when the national average for the entire Forest Service is closer to 65 percent in 1991."

Claiming that he is "shocked" by what is happening to the U.S. Forest Service, Mumma denies that he is in any way a radical reformer. Rather, he says, he was caught in a bind created by federally prescribed (though not legally mandated) harvest levels that would have clearly violated environmental and other regulatory measures. The Office of General Counsel within the Department of Agriculture repeatedly advised Mumma and others that existing environmental laws must be followed, even if it meant failing to meet a prescribed quota. "You had a choice," summed up Representative Gerry Sikorski during Mumma's testimony before the Civil Service

Subcommittee in the fall of 1991. "Get the cut out and violate laws, or follow laws and pay with your career."

The spring before Mumma's testimony, Federal District Judge William Dwyer issued an injunction against logging in portions of the Northwest, saying that there was "a deliberate and systematic refusal by the Forest Service and the Fish and Wildlife Service to comply with laws protecting wildlife." Dwyer went on to say that this was not the doing of those at working levels of these agencies, but rather a condition that "reflects decisions made by higher authorities in the executive branch of government."

Offering further evidence of foul play was the 1992 testimony before a House subcommittee of a former Forest Service criminal investigator, who reported that several Northwest national forests were doctoring data to permit illegal cuts in the habitats of endangered species.

In these erratic, uncertain times, there is one thing you can bet the farm on: If the political climate remains as it is now, one day soon we will find ourselves in the middle of a systematic dismantling of a wide range of environmental protection laws, beginning with the Endangered Species Act. (In the case of the northern spotted owl, Secretary of the Department of Interior Manuel Lujan has already pushed hard to waive the provision of the Endangered Species Act requiring the government aid in the bird's recovery.) The bottom line is that the public lands of this country are turning into a golden teat for nursing the cries and whims of an already thoroughly subsidized body of extractive industries. Perhaps the national forest system would be better termed the corporate forest system, and mascot Smoky the Bear traded in for a bright yellow dozer.

After much fruitless searching for the Bitch Creek Trail, I finally give up, pull out the map and compass, and begin walking cross-country. In just under a mile I find forest again, and while the going is definitely rougher here compared to the clear-cuts, the land seems refreshingly animated—the flash of blue grouse running for cover, the hollow drumming of the three-toed woodpecker, the rich, flutey singing of the solitaire.

It is now August 10, and the northern Rocky Mountain summer is in full swing. Young bald eagles, covered in mottled brown and ivory feathers, have learned much about flying since they first dove from the nest in early July. Elk are in their summer ranges high in the mountains, and white-tailed deer fawns, while not yet weaned, are beginning to roam with their mothers through the nooks and crannies of forest. Male mallards have started the molt that will soon cover their heads in striking cloaks of iridescent green. Rabbitbrush is blanketed with yellow discflowers, and the air is filled with sage pollen. Lavender blooms lace the upper stalks of fireweed, while each day acres of whortleberries end up in the mouths of black bears and grizzlies. The earth feels like it is pausing, as if it were unhooking the tether on all the life it has nurtured during the warm, sweet days of early summer. There is a kind of magic in the mountains now. And one of the finest, most bewitching illusions it casts is to make you think that it will never end.

By the time I've walked another two miles, my murky thoughts about logging and politics have started to fade, overwhelmed by views of the deep, timbered gorges of Conant and Coyote canyons. Though the plow and the road have claimed the flat lands lying to the west as far as the eye can see, here on the northern shoulders of the Tetons the country still runs unfettered, urging me into its distant folds like a good wind carrying fire through the forest. On this side of the divide the Tetons do not wear the staggering profile that so distinguishes them from the east, where, bereft of foothills, they rise nearly seven thousand feet straight up into the sky. Yet there is still great appeal in these smoother, more rounded ridges. At the upper heads of many west-slope valleys lie not sawtoothed peaks but flat, strapping mountains, most comprised of horizontal bands of Paleozoic sedimentary rock laid down during an eternity of ancient oceans. Immediately beneath these peaks are long, tumbling reaches of meadow, each flushed with striking blooms of scarlet, lemon, and lavender. And below even those, where streams first gather to begin their runs for the lowlands, are great riparian corridors choked with willow, monkeyflower, and mint.

It is along one of these lower corridors in the Jedediah Smith Wilderness that I find great fields of false hellebore. The broad, glossy leaves cling to stalks that rise above my head, and from a distance they have the look of corn plots in late July. Though toxic, this native plant and its near relatives have held a prominent place in the lives of Native Americans for countless centuries. Shoshone people crushed the root and applied it as a poultice to wounds and poisonous snake bites, a practice first observed in New England tribes during the middle of the seventeenth century. Across much of the country Native American women used a tea made from the root of false hellebore as a contraceptive. (Some tribes reported that this tea could be taken in small quantities on a daily basis if made from fresh roots, but making it from the cured root could cause sterility.) Similarly widespread was the use of the plant as an emetic, which is a drug to induce vomiting. Emetics, incidentally, were long the treatment of choice to relieve indigestion, largely because in many places nature's larders didn't offer much in the way of alternatives; two of the other remedies in this area, sage and mint tea, seem to have only limited effect.

But the most intriguing use of false hellebore was to slow down the heart and lower blood pressure, an effect which is in part induced by the alkaloids jervine and veratridine. While some sources have suggested that early European settlers discovered this fact on their own, it's far more likely that they learned it from the Native Americans, who are thought to have been using the plant for such purposes long before Europeans ever set foot in the New World. The truth is that from the time that colonists stood huddled along the cold, wet shores of New England, until covered wagons rolled westward across the prairies, native peoples routinely provided newcomers with at least general information about the use of native plants: cottonroot tea to ease childbirth, dogwood bark for fevers, pinkroot for intestinal parasites, cascara as a laxative—each piece of advice the result of literally hundreds of years of experimentation. Though some early doctors scoffed at treatments offered by Native Americans, to date more than two hundred of their plant cures have been listed in the United States Pharmacopeia and the National Formulary.

(Understandably, most of these free lessons in pharmacology came to a screeching halt as the newcomers began killing and starving the teachers. By the latter part of the nineteenth century those who would learn about plants in the West could do so only by living with the tribes and gaining their trust; not long after that, most native peoples would share little or nothing of what they knew.)

One of the great challenges of moving along the Tetons is that you must navigate an almost endless series of east–west drainages. This means trudging twelve or fifteen hundred feet up a canyon face, crossing a narrow ridge line, and then making a long drop down into the next drainage, only to repeat the entire cycle when you get to the bottom. For me it means first climbing over Dead Horse Pass into South Badger Creek, then into South Leigh Creek, and then up and over into the South Fork of Teton Creek. I'm pondering all this drainage hopping during lunch at the Granite Basin Lakes. Feeling a bit under the weather, as if the flu were starting to rise, and having already negotiated two of the three aforementioned drainages over the past couple days, I'm not particularly thrilled at the thought of dropping 1,800 feet into South Leigh Creek, and then having to climb a whopping 2,600 feet to the top of the divide that separates it from Teton Creek.

There is another option. If I ascend roughly a thousand feet from Granite Lakes to the southern flank of Littles Peak I can pick up a narrow, choppy granite ridge—the hydrographic crest of the Tetons—snaking along the high, wild western boundary of Grand Teton National Park. A guide told me that this divide becomes extremely difficult to follow the further south it drifts. But if I can just stay with it for two miles, passing the South Leigh Creek drainage at the headwall, I'll miss more than three thousand feet of pounding down and grunting up.

Not that this route isn't without problems. While the weather looks good now, this is still very much the season of afternoon thunderstorms; finding myself atop a ten-thousand-foot exposed ridge during a major cloudburst would be anything but pleasant. Secondly, because of a last-minute mix-up on an order at the map store in Cody, I'm armed only with 1:100,000 scale topographic maps. This means that instead of the landscape being displayed in contour lines separated by forty vertical feet, as I'm used to, here the lines represent spaces of 164 feet—a serious disadvantage when you're trying to make decisions of how best to safely negotiate routes up and over rugged country. It would be entirely conceivable, for example, to strike out across what appears to be fairly navigable landscape, only to find myself standing on the lip of a hundred-foot cliff that never showed up on the map at all.

Finally, pulled by both the appeal of a more direct route, and what I know will be a staggering view into the heart of the Tetons, I pack up and begin the climb toward Littles Peak. There continues to be an almost endless collection of high meadows peppered with granite boulders and brilliant canvases of monkeyflower, elephant head, buttercup, and paintbrush. A couple hundred feet above Granite Lakes is a narrow bench where these flower gardens are broken by still pockets of water the color of the summer sky. One rather sizable pond, completely encircled by wildflowers, hangs on the extreme outer edge of the bench; immediately beyond, the world falls off in a dizzy, 1,600-foot plunge into South Leigh Creek valley.

By the time I near the southern end of Littles Peak, dark clouds are approaching rapidly from the west. Instead of making for the ridge I decide to stay four hundred or so feet below it, hurrying south past great jumbles of rock and ragged, wind-torn conifers, a few of them wearing the black scars of lightning strikes, pausing every twenty yards or so to look over my right shoulder to check the development of the approaching storm. In another thousand yards there's little underfoot but huge fields of talus. Crossing them means making a series of small jumps from one boulder to another, always poised to move off quickly should one of the rocks suddenly give way. I'm already past the point where I should have climbed to the ridge, but now the sky is completely dark, and to the south I can see thin, gray curtains of rain dangling from the bellies of the clouds. I cannot safely risk the ridge, nor do I relish the thought of rock hopping with a full pack on a steep slope of wet boulders. With thunder rumbling overhead, and the first cold drops of rain slapping against my face and legs, I make a hasty retreat to a shallow alcove perched on the edge of oblivion. There is barely enough room for me to squat inside, so I pull maps, compass, and a bag of jerky out of the pack, and, scrambling, find a small overhang thirty feet away where I stash the remainder of the gear.

After fifteen minutes there is still no lightning, so I crawl out of the alcove and take compass sightings of two nearby peaks. Accounting for the difference between true north and magnetic north—here in the Tetons about 17 degrees—I use a straightedge to draw pencil lines on the map from each of the sighted peaks back toward me; where the two lines cross is my current location. Even with a map of this scale, it's easy to see that the headwalls just to the south are so steep as to be impassable; if I'm serious about taking this route, then I'll have to climb to the crest of the ridge.

Thirty minutes later the clouds begin to break above me and to the west, so I shoulder the pack and huff up the remaining four hundred feet to the top. I'm in a hurry, still being somewhat nervous about the weather, but I can't resist stopping every now and then just to stare at the scene before me. Five miles to the southeast, great blankets of cheerless clouds are rolling about the necks of twelve-thousand-foot peaks. More than once I see great bolts of lightning stabbing at the tops of Grand Teton, Middle Teton, and Mount Owen, and I wonder how many climbers are at this very moment hunkered down, hiding from the storm in some narrow crack or crevice in the sheer face of the granite. In a couple of places the crest I'm following is barely six feet across. At each edge are sheer, 1,500-foot drops into a land so full of rock and rubble that it looks like the world fresh out of creation. Lake

Solitude, lying underneath me to the east at the head of Cascade Creek Canyon, is a silent, eerie pocket of dull cobalt blue. Though the French may have likened these mountains to breasts, hence the name Tetons, from where I stand they look far more like something out of the great myths of the Shoshone, who referred to them as the "hoary headed Fathers."

After roughly a mile and a half, the sky now clear overhead but still grumbling to the east, I begin working my way down a steep run of talus into the upper reaches of the South Leigh Lakes Basin. The land here is magnificent in a way that only alpine cirque basins can be. Small streams of whitewater launch off the edges of hundred-foot cliffs, emitting thin hisses as they crash against the jumbles of granite below. In the wake of the spray are blooms of monkeyflowers, buttercups, bluebells, buckwheat, campion, globeflowers, and glacier lilies; from a distance the ground around the falls looks like a dropcloth fresh off the floor of a kindergarten art class, thoroughly spattered with purples, yellows, blues, and ivories.

Everywhere the ground is lined with the twisted dirt casts of pocket gophers—a tiny animal, seldom seen, with tremendous influence on the world of alpine vegetation. The pocket gopher was named for the small pouches located on either side of its jaw, and is into earth-moving in a very big way. Hardly bigger than a good-size deli pickle, it can excavate a hundred feet of underground tunnel in less than twelve hours; over the course of a year (pocket gophers do not hibernate) it will move literally thousands and thousands of pounds of earth. Naturalist Donald Streubel puts the matter into fine persepctive: "Consider what it would be like," he writes, "to excavate five tons of soil per year with two teaspoons."

The dirt that this little digger moves in creating his four- to five-hundred-foot-long, bilevel tunnel system is deposited on the surface of the ground. Then, when excavations are completed, the hole through which the dirt was carried is tightly plugged. In winter pocket gophers will tunnel through the snow and then pack the passageways with excavated dirt. It's these casts, or eskers, as they're sometimes called, that one sees in summer, lying twisted like brown snakes across so much of the high country. Through their activities pocket gophers aerate the soil and impove moisture retention, distribute seeds, and recycle minerals—processes that to a large extent would simply not get done without them, since the alpine world is almost totally without burrowing creatures of any kind, including worms.

The upper runs of the pocket gopher's burrow system lie just far enough underground for the animal to collect roots, tubers, and stems during excavation, many of which he will transport, via those fur-lined pockets in his cheeks, to a variety of underground storage chambers. Some hikers have been startled to see a trailside plant suddenly sink out of sight right before their eyes—a clear sign of a pocket gopher at work. Grizzlies make good use of the animal's efforts, never hesitating to tear up a pocket gopher's tunnel system for a chance to raid his larders.

From my campsite I can see vast fields of barley and alfalfa lying to the west, past the entrance to South Leigh Creek Canyon. Near the mouth of the chasm the fields look like the blocks of a vast patchwork quilt. Farther to the west—twenty miles, thirty miles away—they begin to fuse together, until at last there is just one long, soft wash of jade spilling into the evening sun. At that distant point the landscape is no longer seen in terms of farms per se, with barns and houses and tractors, but merely as vague patterns and textures sketched across the smooth face of the earth. It's certainly true, as Thompson Campbell wrote in 1799, that distance lends enchantment to the view. And that enchantment is more than reason enough to climb mountains.

The rich lowlands to the west also cradle the slow meanderings of the Teton River, flowing through a green, fertile basin known to early nineteenth-century trappers as Pierre's Hole. Named for an Iroquois employee of the Hudson Bay Company who was killed here by Blackfeet Indians, this was a favorite stomping ground for many in the fur trade. Trapper Osborne Russell wrote of Pierre's Hole as being thickly cloaked with grass and forbs, and abounding with buffalo, elk, deer, and antelope.

In 1832 a rendezvous held here—one of fourteen total—was marked by what some have described as a "rousing" battle with the Gros Ventre Indians. Rendezvous were annual gatherings where trappers and Indians met with traders' caravans from the eastern settlements, and they were unique to the Rocky Mountains. Indians traded furs, buffalo robes, horses, buckskin clothing, and dried meat for such things as cheap smoothbore muskets (the whites kept the good rifles for themselves), cooking utensils, tobacco, rum, rings, and silver hawk bells. Trappers, on the other hand, exchanged beaver pelts, which for a time were worth about five dollars each, as well as other furs for the equipment they'd need for the coming year. (Free trappers, who were not affiliated with companies, could expect to spend a good twelve to fifteen dollars apiece just for traps.)

Whatever surplus cash or credit anyone had was quickly and thoroughly invested in one of the biggest free-for-alls these mountains have ever seen. There were great assemblages of Indians in festive, colorful dress. Gun blasts from shooting matches could be heard throughout the day, and once everyone was thoroughly soused, a few marksmen moved on to dueling in the dark. There were wrestling matches and stick games, and always the smell of wild game dripping over the cook fires. There were packs of barking dogs, and the thunder of racing horses, not to mention an endless array of fighting, storytelling, and sexual romps. And always, it seemed, there was waking up at dawn in the tall grass still drunk, or at least very hung over. When the rendezvous was over the Indians headed back to their encampments, the trappers went into the hills, and the traders left for the settlements. In the short span of twenty years the fashionable beaver felt hat yielded to silk, and the beaver itself was all but exterminated from the Rocky Mountains. And rendezvous dried up and blew away.

Tonight the sky is clean and clear, and when full darkness finally comes I can stand at the edge of this basin and look down into a lake filled with stars. To my good fortune the

Perseids meteor shower is running tonight, and these lights too can be seen skating across the surface of the water. The only sound is the steady ripple of the outlet stream, as well as an occasional outburst of song from a pack of coyotes hanging out in the black forests of the valley floor. Once in bed I try to make a few notes, but I get very little done before the weight of the day's efforts, combined with whatever flu bug I happen to have, pull me down into bed and off to sleep.

The next morning, while eastbound toward Fred's Mountain, I hear what seems to be a very young coyote yipping weakly in the forest far below, as if he were hurt. I try moving down the slope in his direction, but each time I advance any distance he becomes quiet, only to start up again when I move back up the slope. It has been a good month now since this fellow and his two or three siblings were weaned and left the den to learn to hunt. At first they concentrated on fat mice and ground squirrels, and perhaps an occasional hunk of carrion. But as the remainder of the summer wears on they'll be forced to supplement their diets with insects and berries. It's interesting that the coyote holds such a prominent position in the myths of almost all Rocky Mountain Native American cultures; the fact is you simply could not have sat around the winter fires of any Shoshone, Gros Ventre, Bannock, Blackfeet, Flathead, Kalispell, or Crow camp without hearing tale after tale being told about the exploits, tricks, or heroic deeds of Coyote. Yet in our culture we've taken exactly the opposite stance, having spent astonishing amounts of money trying to obliterate the poor beast with rifles, traps, cyanide guns, and 1080-type poison stations. In 1990 alone the Animal Damage Control Bureau spent 26 million dollars in Western states, most of it to kill about 75,000 coyotes. Still the animal's numbers remain high, a testimony to both their intelligence and their almost uncanny instinct for survival.

The war against coyotes has always been a private one, waged by a powerful ranching community. But that's not to say there aren't some ranchers who admire this animal, one reason being that he's very adept at keeping a lid on populations of mice, ground squirrels, and rabbits—all of which eat valuable forage. Perhaps the difference of opinion toward the critter can be traced to the fact that there have always been those ranchers who saw the Western landscape as a battleground, while others had a deep if somewhat reserved appreciation of its wild nature. Maybe this is why in one old tune from the open range we hear a cowpoke sing:

Oh bury me not on the lone prairie
Where the wild coyotes will howl o'er me.

While another cowboy makes a completely different request:

Oh, bury me out on the prairie,
Where the coyotes may howl o'er my grave

I try a couple more times to get close to this little yipper, but he will have none of if. In the end all I can do is call down to him a wish for luck and good pickings through the winter, and resume my trek westward along the ridge. I'm trying to pick up a trail that switchbacks downward two thousand feet into the North Fork of Teton Creek. But while the path is easy to find at first, it soon peters out into a thick weave of vegetation, leaving me to comb the mountainside looking for it. (Again, the large-scale map proves to be my undoing.) With twelve miles yet to go and my energy waning, I finally give up and head straight down the steep flank of the mountain cross-country, a route that pummels my knees until they feel like the caps will blow right off. By the time I reach Teton Campground it is three o'clock; I'm weak and nauseated, my feet hurt, and I have eight miles yet to go to reach my campsite in the Alaska Basin.

There have been occasions when I've resented the quick pace at which this entire trek has unfolded, and right now is one of them. Over the last two days alone I've passed an incredible array of dramatic side canyons and cool aspen draws, delightful waterfalls and quiet, glistening lakes—any of which I would have loved to have gotten to know better. Initially I was reconciled to the pace of these five hundred miles because I assured myself that at the end I'd at least have a decent list of places to go back to and explore further. But already the list is the length of my leg, one special place melting into yet another, and I'm not even out of the Tetons! Curiously, my frustration at not getting to know specific places is growing in direct proportion to my ability to sense the spectacle of the connected whole. I'm continually surprised at how well this ecosystem hangs together—a single body with blood made of fire and fish, birds, mammals and insects, flowing up and down the veins of valleys and ridge tops, through all its myriad appendages. To be in one place is in a sense to be in the entire system. The notion of treating a single strand of a web like the Yellowstone Rockies as if it could somehow stand alone is ludicrous, akin to ripping a hundred pages out of a thousand-page novel, and then claiming that only 10 percent of the story was affected.

It's nearly dark by the time I reach the basin. Even so, I can see that this is staggering country—a flat, ice-scoured sink dappled with water pockets and beautiful granite islands, most of them sitting in a sea of alpine wildflowers. To the east, along the hydrographic divide, the flattopped mountains seem even larger than those farther to the north—giant ships and mammoth battlements frozen against the alpen glow. Even though there are several camps in the vicinity, the basin is as quiet as a church. I hear little but the occasional titters of white-crowned sparrows, and see nothing stirring but a fat yellow-bellied marmot waddling up a chunk of granite. It's as if everyone is hunkered down, talking in whispers, trying their best not to break the spell of this perfect summer night.

It's hard for most of us to even imagine what life is like for much of the year along these high, wild rooftops. Winter temperatures often plunge to thirty and forty below zero, and snow may accumulate to depths of twenty feet. The wind can blow a remarkably bitter tune, frequently gusting to speeds of over one hundred miles per hour. For decades scientists had a great deal of trouble even studying these regions, since it was nearly impossible to find instruments that would perform reliably under such severe conditions. Typically it's not until the second week in July that summer finally comes to the alpine reaches of the high country; by Labor Day, it has already started drifting out of reach.

For most of the creatures that make their homes here, survival depends not only on being hardy, but also on being efficient, and able to run a strong, swift race against a fleeting summer. Whereas plants found down in the valleys don't typically produce root material until the temperature reaches roughly forty-five degrees, most alpine plants are up and at it as soon as the temperature nudges above the freezing mark. Likewise, many young mammals living at lower altitudes, such as deer, spend the first weeks of their lives highly dependent on their parents. A young bighorn sheep or Rocky Mountain goat, on the other hand, is remarkably agile at just three days old. By the time five days have passed they can dance and play among a tangle of sheer cliffs and bluffs that would leave most of us in a state of utter vertigo.

Fur is also generally thicker and deeper on animals of the high country, while feathers—the most efficient insulators of all—tend to be of a more efficient design. The real trick here is not warmth per se, but how to keep warm in the winter without burning up in the summer. The solution usually involves a blend of eating, panting, preening, and moulting. The one bird who lives year round on the tundra, the white-tailed ptarmigan, survives the hundred-degree temperature spreads by going through three different sets of feathers.

As you might imagine, plant growth occurs at a rate that could confound the patience of Job. Over the course of its first year of growth, the tiny alpine buttercup manages to produce only a single cell. This cell divides during the second growing season, produces a bud during the third, and finally, after four years, sends out a bright yellow bloom about the size of a thumbtack. The beautiful moss campion, on the other hand, may need a quarter of a century to reach a spread of seven inches. Largely due to the vicious winds, what trees there are on the tundra tend to hug the ground like landlubbers just off a stormy sea voyage. Such growth is called *krummholz,* a German word that means "elfin timber." And elfin it is; a three-hundred-year-old limber pine probably won't reach above your waist, with a trunk that measures no more than three inches across.

There are actually dozens of plants in these alpine gardens that you would recognize from lower altitudes, though you might have to get down on your hands and knees to find them (biologists call them belly plants). Small plants with short stems require less energy, and therefore time, to produce, and are also more likely to escape the abrasion and drying effects of the wind. Furthermore, many ground-hugging plants are able to use their folds of tiny leaves as heat traps—so much so, in fact, that the temperature inside the leaf mat may be fifteen or twenty degrees warmer than the air surrounding it. These "cushion plants," as they're often called, also tend to trap bits of leaves and other debris that blow by, which over time will help raise the level of the soil underneath. This is a painstakingly slow process: Some researchers have estimated that alpine soil is built at a rate of about an inch every thousand years.

It's this slow pace of regeneration that makes the tundra so fragile. The impact from even a few hikers can take decades to heal, and even then, success at revegetating disturbed areas has been marginal at best. The need to protect alpine tundra extends far beyond purely aesthetic reasons. Throughout the West, a tremendous percentage of the total moisture produced by watersheds is regulated by vegetation found above timberline. The alpine tundra of Colorado, for example, makes up a mere 3.5 percent of the state's total land mass, yet produces a full 20 percent of the stream flow. (It's been estimated that in the arid lands west of the hundredth meridian, every acre of elevated mountain land—not tundra per se—produces irrigation, industrial and agricultural water for six acres of lowland. This means that the Yellowstone ecosystem alone is generating enough water to supply an area roughly the size of England and Wales.)

Alpine vegetation also helps maintain soil stability; were these plants not here, many places would experience a much higher number of landslides. And finally, the atmosphere at high elevations contains substantially higher levels of radio-activity than are found down low. Some of this radiation is collected by falling snow—the same snow, of course, that forms the headwaters of most major river systems. To a significant extent, the complex network of tiny plants that live above the timberline filter out these radioactive substances, removing them before they reach the farms, homes, and industries of more populated areas.

My trip the next morning across the Static Peak Divide—at 10,800 feet the highest point on any maintained hiking trail in the Tetons—is extraordinary. Were it my particular mission to find the home of the mountain gods, I would need go no further than this. Buck Mountain and Static Peak loom beside the trail like the portals of a netherworld. Remnant patches of snow lie among enormous jumbles of talus and stony rubble, images that would seem to suggest disintegration not by small swells of ice and thin lines of running water, but by some incredible explosion on the top of the world. Gray clouds race in from the west and take the summits into their folds, as if they were exchanging something secret in the embrace, and then vanish right before my eyes.

"On the mountains there is freedom!" wrote Friedrich von Schiller. But there is also shock and astonishment. And it is served up in doses quite sufficient to refire the burned-out brain, to squeeze new blood into the tissue of a shrinking heart.

TEN

If your particular version of heaven happens to include mountains, then you just might find yourself kicking off life after life at the foot of some place like the Tetons. This is the quintessential vision of the high country, appearing in lusty, twelve-thousand-foot steeples of gneiss and schist and feldspar. They are to mountains what the Grand Canyon is to gorges; what Chartres is to cathedrals; what dark chocolate is to desserts.

Yet directly to the east, across the shining waters of the Snake River, past the long sweeps of grass and sage that lay thick and shaggy across the floor of Jackson Hole, is another range of mountains—the Gros Ventre. By comparison the landscape here is subdued, marked not by dramatic peaks but by rolling mountains and easy, lilting meadows. There are very few lakes, little opportunity for major mountain climbing, and no dizzy cascades plunging from the lips of hanging glacial valleys. Hikers who are looking for gusto, those seeking that certain rush that comes in the stony turrets of the high country, do not come here. Many of the trails are faint, and often peter out altogether, leaving you to make your way with map in hand, marking your position by noting the gentle divides you cross, or by counting the number of side streams passed on the way up some endless run of valley.

But to me the Gros Ventre seem equally alluring, a place where, with the exception of hunting season, you can drift day after day in relative solitude, a landscape not so much to conquer as to embrace.

It was a group of Plains Indians who first tried to explain to French trappers that the tribes of these lands were always hungry—a sign made by passing both hands over the stomach. But the trappers, who were never any good at charades, interpreted this as an indication that the people had big bellies, or "gros ventres." Like many tribes in the northern Rockies, the Gros Ventre didn't appreciate intrusions by outsiders who were hellbent for beaver pelts. In the course of forty years of the fur trade, from roughly 1805 to 1845, close to 20 percent of all trappers are thought to have met their deaths at the hands of warriors from seven tribes, one of which was the Gros Ventre.

Despite the magnificence of Grand Teton and the luster of Yellowstone, it is these peripheral lands that make this place whole, that keep the national park islands from becoming altogether artificial ecosystems. From a biological standpoint these runs of valley and forest have not only a complex assortment of plant and animal dynamics, but also serve as important migration corridors for everything from elk to moose to birds. In addition, they're a critically important component of the region's watersheds.

Land like this can also be psychologically important. While as a kid I spent most of my time dreaming of the craggy Teton highlines depicted in Wyoming travel brochures, I sensed even then that the glory of those peaks was somehow amplified by the wild waves and ripples of the low country spreading from their feet. If the mystery of the mountains overwhelmed the senses, then the mystery of the adjacent lowlands seemed to nourish them. If the high country shouted, the low country whispered. Trying to protect just the dramatic mountain lands, or in the case of Yellowstone Park, an exotic cluster of geyser basins, is like a conductor deciding to skip the first hour and a half of Handel's *Messiah* because he knows what the audience enjoys most is the "Hallelujah Chorus."

When I was eighteen a friend and I drove out of the Midwest cornfields and across the high plains in a 1964 Pontiac Tempest, bound for the Colorado Rockies. On the prairie I had an almost overwhelming urge to stop the car and just walk off into the middle of nondescript nowhere. I didn't, because at the time there seemed for both of us a certain urgency to hurry on to timberline. But now it occurs to me that it's the life pouring out of the more subtle nooks and crannies of the land that form the most accessible connections to the psyche—the smell of willow sap, the color of watercress under a sheet of stream water, the way a chickadee fluffs his feathers against the winter cold. The simpler, plainer pieces of woodland and prairie are the places that you first love as a child, and then not again until you're old enough to recall that you once found something special there, something of the utmost importance.

After 125 miles of solo time Jane is back on the trail with me, and we slip into the wilds via Horsetail Creek, pushing slowly upward into a land of long, timber-capped ridges and russet-colored scarps. It feels good to be together again, back to the rhythm of the trail—the setting and striking of camp, the daylong drifts across the terrain, the conversations that rise in the middle of nearly every afternoon. Thirteen years ago we spent our first summer together wandering through the Sawtooth Range of Idaho, giving each other bunches of wildflowers stuffed into empty beer cans, breakfasting in the backcountry on fresh trout and fireweed tea. The following year we were married in those mountains, in a meadow bursting with camas lily; the night of our wedding I carried Jane not across the threshold of a house or a hotel room, but through the open sliding door of a Chevy Van camper. Since then there hasn't been a single period in our lives not marked by long twists of trail or dusty back roads.

Such movement is good for us. In our worst of times we've never found anything so helpful as merely taking to the countryside. The same anger and agitation that at home can fester for days comes and goes out here with relative ease. Of course some of that has to do with the fact that sweating up a mountain trail tends to take the hostility right out of you. But it also seems that as the open land washes through us it's somehow able to clean the cuts and make them heal. Anger may rise here, but it rarely consumes.

The rolling landscape we're walking through this morning is shaky, unstable country, prone to massive slumps and slides. On a cool, moist morning in June of 1925, from a point well up on a high ridge cradling the south side of the Gros Ventre River, a slab of earth a mile long and a third of a mile wide suddenly broke free from its tenuous moorings, plowed into and across the river, and rolled part way up the rock wall on the other side of the valley. As a similar, though much smaller and slower event happened years earlier several miles upstream, creating Upper Slide Lake, the body of water formed behind this new plug of earth and rubble was called Lower Slide Lake. Less than two years after Lower Slide Lake was created, a portion of the natural dam that braced it suddenly gave way, loosing an immense wall of water into the small village of Kelly, located six miles downstream, killing half a dozen people.

Some geologists believe that the land here is so fragile because the mountains are still settling; as sheets of soft rock are dissolved by ground moisture, the surface collapses. Others argue that great masses of glacial ice are still buried deep in the ground, and as these melt the surrounding soils become saturated. This eventually loosens unstable rock foundations, until the ground above them finally gives way.

It's hardly surprising that such dramatic land movements would show up in the myths of Native Americans. One Gros Ventre story tells how long ago there was in the vicinity of the 1925 slide an enormous cave, inside of which was a beautiful valley thick with grass and wood and water. Yet even with all these riches people didn't often frequent the cave, since they couldn't go far before it became dark and difficult to travel. One day a group of hunters were out looking for buffalo, and the sun suddenly vanished—perhaps due to a major eclipse—slipping the entire region into total darkness. Fearing that the sun had disappeared for good, the people retreated into the great cave, bringing with them a small herd of buffalo.

After they'd gone some distance a great slide occurred, closing off the entrance to the cave. It is said that not only do these Gros Ventres still live inside the mountain, but that the buffalo they first brought with them have grown into an enormous herd. When you feel the earth tremble, when landslides occur on the outer face of the mountain, it is because there's a buffalo hunt going on inside, with thousands of black hooves pounding through the inner valleys.

The 1,500-foot climb along Horsetail Creek is remarkably quiet. In fact, the two men riding mountain bikes we pass about two miles from the trailhead are the last people we will see in almost forty miles of walking. Several of the drainages here are flanked by gentle, open hills quilted with sage and aspen, the branches of the latter framing the parapets of the Tetons, which rise like the gates of enchantment through the bright blue skies to the west. When the pack trail we're on makes a fork that isn't shown on our maps, we take a wild guess and turn east. But within a mile it fades out altogether, and so we are trekking cross-country once again, dropping across broad fingers of land covered in weaves of pine, spruce, and aspen. Some of the nooks contain seeps of spring water, giving rise to rich mats of sedge. And everywhere there are beautiful carpets of wildflowers—blooms of columbine and bluebells dangling in the shade, and paintbrush and yarrow rising from the meadows that lie open to the sun.

Yarrow is known to most as a rather ho-hum weed—dull, feathery leaves and umbels of small, rather ordinary-looking ivory- to pink-colored flowers. Yet few weeds have the illustrious history of this one. Its genus name, Achillea, is a reference to the great Greek warrior Achilles, who rose to fame storming the city of Troy around 1200 B.C. During that battle, Achilles is said to have relied heavily on yarrow to treat the wounds of his soldiers—a practice he learned from the famous centaur physician, Chiron. And a good practice it was. Yarrow leaves do in fact help control bleeding, prevent infection by killing bacteria, and even contain substances that act as a limited local anesthetic.

In the years following the Trojan War, records suggest that both Greek and Roman soldiers carried yarrow with them as a part of their regular supplies. (When the Gauls invaded the Roman Empire, included in the spoils were stores of yarrow.) And still other warriors followed. Knights of the Middle Ages relied on yarrow for treating wounds of the lance and sword, and Civil War troops referred to it as soldier's woundwort. The Ute Indians knew the plant as "wound medicine." Another nickname, carpenter's grass, suggests that yarrow may have once been used in treating the cuts and scrapes of woodworkers. Over the centuries people have also tried to use yarrow for treating everything from ulcers to dysentery, flatulence to depression. In England it was once said that if picked from the grave of a young man, yarrow would bring maidens a vision of their future lovers.

Given the long and frequent use of yarrow by the masses, it doesn't come as much of a surprise that somewhere along the line the Christian church would associate it with evil. This is precisely what happened in England during the seventeenth century, at a time when hundreds of women folk healers were being carted off and hung as witches. Despite its proven curative powers, in those days yarrow became known by the rather unflattering name of "devil's plaything." Yarrow is still used in France as a complexion wash, in Norway to help anesthetize toothaches, and is one component in a new drug being used to treat hepatitis. Scientists in Lithuania are looking into the plant for its potential in limiting the growth of tumors, while here in the United States researchers are testing it for use in controlling mosquitoes.

All of this brings to mind the by now familiar notion of saving ecosystems because of the useful medicines they might one day offer. In modern times we tend to forget that over a quarter of all drugs issued by our pharmacies still contain drugs actually taken from plants, while most of the rest are synthetic copies, to which minor modifications may have been made. Because it's more costly to develop a drug directly from a plant than to synthesize one, until recently American pharmaceutical companies have focused almost all of their attention on manipulating the chemical structures of their synthetic copies. The problem with this is that when you cut plants out of the picture, you also cut out the chance of discovering entirely new chemicals, some of which might well have applications to what are currently untreatable diseases. This point has been driven home again and again: with a derivative from the may apple used in the chemotherapy of small cell lung cancer, with digitalis from the purple foxglove to treat congestive heart failure, and most recently, with taxol from the Pacific yew, now being used with great success in the treatment of ovarian cancer.

A problem with the taxol of the Pacific yew—one that will almost certainly show up with other plants later on—is that the compound is so complex that scientists fear they'll never be able to synthesize it. As an alternative, researchers are trying to extract the material using cultures of individual cells, similar to the way that insulin is harvested from bacterial cells. Given enough time and resources, such efforts are likely to succeed. The question that remains, however, is how many other potentially significant treatments and cures will have been lost in the meantime through the careless destruction of our public forests?

When we finally stumble out onto a tumble of sage-covered hills above Slate Creek, we're clearly not where we thought we'd be. Nor is the terrain variant enough to show up very well in the contour lines of our topo maps. The specific east–west drainage we're looking for could be up the creek, or it could be down, and guessing wrong might result in a major detour. On top of all this, it's fairly late in the day, thick gray blankets of rain clouds are building like layer cakes to the west, and we're both tired enough to be dangerously short on humor.

We spend a good thirty minutes scanning the horizon like two lost sailors groping for an island, but for all our efforts, none of what we see is enough to pinpoint our location. Our best guess is that our connecting drainage lies to the north, but we head south first toward what looks to be a distinct vantage point, about a mile away. Sure enough, when we reach this point it's fairly easy to verify that our route lies back the other direction—a clear case of having guessed right and not feeling one bit good about it. We manage close to three miles heading back north, and with rain on the way call it quits on the grassy flats of a streamside meadow. Since standing around after a long day of hiking tends to erode one's courage, we waste no time jumping into a deep plunge pool along the west bank of Slate Creek. Next the tent goes up, we toss down a few bites of cheese and French bread, and hang the food bag in a branch of an old Douglas fir snag as the first raindrops begin to pelt the campsite. The last thing either of us remembers is lying in the tent listening to the ring of a good downpour drumming on the tent fly—a soothing, monotone lullaby that, along with the sound of creek water licking at the smooth rocks, puts us out like candles in the wind.

The next two days are a graceful coast, five and six-mile-long runs of bright meadow alternating with dense patches of spruce-fir forest, dark and rich and full of mystery. One narrow valley, framed on either side by almost impenetrable timber, is completely flooded by beaver workings, leaving us to trade our boots for river sandals and then muck through a hundred yards of calf-deep mud. In several meadows the trail disappears under lush mats of vegetation, forcing us to pick our own routes across the countryside. Throughout it all, we walk utterly alone.

Originally inspired by the need to scan the terrain ahead for grizzlies, I've made a game out of trying to pick up the slightest animal movements nearby—the hop of a hermit thrush, the black, glossy ears of a moose calf walking through the willow thickets. In the mornings my vision and hearing seem especially well tuned to the surroundings, and in those times the land seems to be overflowing with life, full of hum and warble and flutter. Deep in the forest a deer flicks her tail, or a red-tailed hawk ruffles his neck feathers from his perch high in a Douglas fir. A red squirrel twitches his tail, and a deer mouse dashes across the trail. A flycatcher lets out a faint peep, horseflies buzz, trout gulp mosquitoes from a quiet pool. A small snake hurries through the grass. It dawns on me that for people living full-time with the land—dedicated nomads, if you will—the world must take on a profoundly different cast, a seamless flow of relationships in which it would be impossible to imagine any single component unhinged from the whole. There are many who have mastered the names and the habits of nature. But who among us is left with the sagacity to feel the rhythm of it all, to grasp the heady, blurring spin of creation?

In a thin twist of open meadow we stumble across an old dirt-floored line shack, still being used by the cowboys of the local cattlemen's association. Most line shacks are snapshots of the bare necessities in the life of a working cowboy, and this one is no exception. There are three plywood bunks hugging walls of rough-cut timber, as well as a couple of worn-out chairs, an old wood stove, tin cups and plates, a soup kettle and a black iron skillet, can opener, flashlight with dead batteries, silverware, matches, Coleman lantern, a variety of tools, and a few old horseshoes.

The pantry is a crooked shelf next to the stove, and it holds two cans of Wagonmaster brand pork and beans, three cans of corn, and a couple cans of green peas. As for reading material, there are several old issues of *Field and Stream*, *People*, and of course, *Western Horseman*. (As you might expect, cowboys are rather fond of horse magazines. At a ranch Jane and I once caretook, the very finest drawings from the pages from *Quarter Horse Journal* had been carefully lifted from the staple bindings and used to decorate the inside wall of the outhouse.) As usual, pervading the entire cabin is the pungent odor of deer mice. There are mousetraps set around the floor and on the window ledge, but the bait is dried nearly to dust. Given how difficult it must be to keep mice out of a place like this, the effort seems to have deteriorated into a mere gesture, like trying to scare blackbirds from your garden by putting up a fake owl.

●

The only unsettling time of our long amble through the Gros Ventre comes late one afternoon as we work our way up Maverick Draw. Storm clouds have built to the point that the entire sky is stained in a bleak wash of sooty gray. Thunder growls and rumbles above us, and the forest, thick with Engelmann spruce and subalpine fir, is gloomy beyond all hope. And then, in the soft mud of a creek crossing we spot the freshest, most formidable grizzly track I have ever seen. The rear foot looks to be nearly eleven inches long, while the front pad is close to six inches. The claw marks are long and clean, and some of the mud is actually still settling around the outer edges. If I had to guess, I'd say that we missed this particular bear by no more than thirty minutes.

The fact that this bruin was going the opposite direction from us is clearly a comfort, yet every time the cold wind slaps us in the face or the sky lets loose with another explosion of thunder, I get very nervous. If I were a god, after all, these would be exactly the kinds of props I'd use to kick off a major ordeal for a couple of hapless mortals trudging through my mountains. As we cross through blind willow thickets we do our very best to make noise, flipping the bells on our packs and talking loudly about nothing at all, like two fools hard of hearing out for an afternoon stroll. In most places there are no climbing trees within easy reach. This means that should we be charged we'd have to drop the packs and try the old act-dead-in-the-fetal-position trick, though I can hardly help but question my ability to play possum with a six-hundred-pound grizzly roughing me up, opening deep cuts in my shoulders and legs with his teeth and claws. A mile from the first track we find a large pile of scat in the trail, a plate-sized mound containing a few bones from a mouse or pocket gopher, some currant seeds, and lots of brown husks from the nuts of whitebark pine.

Not helping my outlook any is the story—told by a man who drove shuttle for us from Jackson Hole—about his friends surprising a female grizzly and two cubs in this exact area, not two months ago. As the female began trotting toward them they fired off a can of pepper spray, but the wind happened to be blowing such that it came dangerously close to flying back in their faces. (I think it's fairly safe to say that the very last position you would want to find yourself in with a bear running toward you is to be flailing around utterly blinded by capsicum, kicking and screaming in agony. You might as well spread some bacon fat on your chest, lie down in the trail, and call the family over for breakfast.) Next they tried to scare Mama Bear off by firing a handgun into the air, but, as often happens, that didn't work at all. Finally, as the bear launched into a full-blown charge they shot her in the shoulder, whereupon she let out a scream and then turned and fled. Despite an extensive ground search and several flyovers by the Fish and Game Department, the bear was never seen again. All this makes me think if I do see a grizzly here, I certainly hope she isn't limping.

It's a relief to enter the more open country at the head of the draw, though by this point we are plodding on through thin sheets of rain. Finally we give in to the weather and hunker underneath a cluster of big subalpine fir; it takes an hour for the rain to let up, and when it does we waste no time scrambling for the top of the pass. We've already come twelve miles, and from the head of this divide it's another five miles down Split Rock Creek to the Togwotee Pass Road. No sooner do we get started down this final stretch when the rain—much colder now, it seems—begins to fall in buckets, quickly turning these bentonite soils the consistency of wagon grease. We have to literally slide down the inclines, and there are times when the bottoms of our boots are coated with enormous clods of dark, slippery mud, some of which flips off the heel onto our legs and packs with every step. We have good rain gear, but the wind drives the drops into every opening, numbing our faces, our hands, and our feet. When we get to stream crossings we no longer bother finding rocks to hop, but plow through in the straightest line possible, grateful for the chance to wash the sludge off our boots.

This is among the longest two hours either of us have ever spent on the trail, and when our old blue Chevy van finally appears through the sheets of the downpour, it feels like we're coming home to the Hilton. After peeling off our rain- and mud-soaked clothes, we dry off, change clothes, and waste no time speeding westward down the highway to the Hatchet Cafe. There, in a green Naugahyde booth by a picture window, we order steaming plates of fried chicken, potatoes, vegetables, and rolls, wolf it down like we haven't eaten in a week, and then top it off with two of the finest slices of cherry and apple pie à la mode this side of the hundredth meridian. Finally, for the first time in nearly seven hours, the cold and rain—and the grizzlies—seem far away.

We have one layover day in which to dry out equipment, wash our clothes and reload the packs, and then travel three hours to a point thirty miles west of Cody, where we'll meet a friend driving our second vehicle. After dropping this car off at our takeout point on Elk Fork, all of us will drive south back to the Togwotee Pass Road, where Jane and I will hit the trail once again the following morning. This leg of the journey will carry us through one of the largest, wildest unroaded areas left in the continental United States. In sixty-five miles of walking, much of it through serious grizzly country, we will neither see nor cross a single road.

When we meet up with Wynn about six o'clock in the evening, he has an old friend with him, David, a book buyer from Greenwich Village who's come west for a change of scenery. By the time we eat dinner and make our way back into the park, a full moon is on the rise, showering the rough-cut peaks of the Absarokas in a flood of silky light. At Yellowstone Lake we stop for a break, and David, fresh out of LaGuardia barely six hours earlier, crawls out of the van one shade short of disbelief, gaping at a vast, silent stretch of water rimmed by dark spires of spruce and fir. As if that were not shocking enough, forty-five minutes later we run down to the shore of Jackson Lake. Behind us, the highway is completely quiet. Straight ahead the full face of the Tetons tower seven thousand feet into the night sky, each nook and cranny bathed in a cast of chalky light that seems straight out of the mists of

Avalon. "Wow," says the usually taciturn, sophisticated David, shaking his head back and forth. "This is incredible." We spend the night at a stock camp in Turpin Meadows. Jane and I are in the van, and Wynn and David have tossed their sleeping bags out on the open ground. Unbeknownst to any of us we are very close to a trail, and the wake-up call at seven the next morning comes in the form of a wrangler passing right by Wynn and David, trailing a dozen pack horses and mules to hunting camps further up country. David hasn't found his glasses yet, and appears to be squinting up at the scene as if he'd just woken up in the middle of a Marlboro commercial. Jane and I look at each other and smile, knowing that whatever worries David may have brought with him from the big city have by now probably been overwhelmed, lost in the smell of pine and leather and horse flesh, and globs of manure dropping onto the trail not twenty feet from his head.

By eight-thirty Jane and I are off again, winding up a ten-mile run of long brown meadows. The trail is lined with fine patches of strawberries, fireweed, asters, and monkeyflowers, and the high, rocky ridgelines are draped in tattered blankets of conifer. Sandhill cranes flute and flutter up the valleys, and the tracks and droppings of elk and deer are everywhere. We find both Swainson's and red-tailed hawks around almost every bend of the trail, tracing easy, open arcs in the late summer sky.

Also hanging in the sky are several light planes, a couple of which are clearly running grid patterns over the mountains below. In all likelihood these are hunting outfitters, or perhaps even hunters themselves, scoping the land to find elk before opening day. I realize that people pay several thousand dollars for a good elk hunt, and that an outfitter's future business depends to a great extent on word of mouth from satisfied customers. Yet the whole idea of pinpointing herds by air so that you can lead a bunch of dudes right to them seems like a cheap shot, an artificial fix that allows those without enough skill or motivation to have more success than they deserve.

We don't come upon a single human footprint on this entire stretch of trail, but horsemen have been here by the hundreds.

And in this wet year, they have been heavy on the land. North Fork Meadows looks like a kind of wilderness expressway— eight and sometimes nine worn, muddy trails lying side by side, running up the valley mile after mile. And most of the traffic is yet to come, when hunters will pour up these draws like freeway commuters at the start of a three-day weekend. Curiously, though, when we ask one outfitter how business is shaping up, he says it's way off. "In Wyoming out-of-staters have to apply for hunting permits in February," he explains, "which is when the Gulf War was going on. I guess everyone was just too spooked to make any long-range plans."

On the second day out we pass the sweeping marshes and meadows that cradle Two Ocean Pass. This is a gentle, peaceful place where a single small creek splits into two separate channels, one bound for the Pacific, and the other for the Gulf of Mexico. Here it's possible for a trout with itchy fins to cross the Continental Divide without the least bit of struggle. Before the government began stocking programs in the region in 1889, obstacles like waterfalls on the Lewis, Gardiner, Falls, and Firehole rivers kept fish from reaching many of Yellowstone's western waterways. Yet in Yellowstone Lake, as well as in the upper and some lower portions of the river, could be found a type of cutthroat whose original home was in the Snake River, on the other side of the Continental Divide. The fish reached these waters, scientists later discovered, by swimming across the divide at Two Ocean Pass.

From about 1823 through 1840, Two Ocean Pass was the route used most often by fur trappers traveling from Jackson Hole to the rich braid of waterways that line the Yellowstone Plateau. So popular was this corridor that a portion of it became known as the Thoroughfare. Jim Bridger himself is thought to have been the first newcomer to see and name Two Ocean Pass, something that he always took a great deal of pride in, despite the fact that few people outside of his own gnarly fraternity ever believed him. "Poets have sung of the meeting of the waters," wrote trapper Osborne Russell during a visit to the pass in 1835. "But the parting of the waters and fish crossing mountains I believe remains unsung as yet by all except the solitary trapper, who sits under the shade of a spreading pine whistling blank verse and beating time to the tune with a whip on his trap sack . . ."

We amble for five miles along Atlantic Creek, the extensive marshes slowly giving way to broad licks of dry meadow, and those finally pinching off into a narrow ravine skirting the fire-scarred thumb of Yellowstone Point. While it was clear from the topo maps that past this point we would join the massive, gaping meadows that frame the twists and turns of the upper reaches of the Yellowstone River, we're completely unprepared for how expansive they really are. Although the timbered crests that frame this colossal valley have been burned from top to bottom, the fluted bones of the mountains laid bare, the place is still astonishing. For nearly thirty miles the Yellowstone River meanders through these immense sun-drenched meadows, each dappled with clusters of willow and enormous sheets of sedge, reedgrass, mountain asters, pussytoes, and bistort.

The Shoshone and Bannock people had an interesting myth to explain the creation of both the Yellowstone River and the Snake, which rises just eleven miles to the west. A long time ago, so the story says, there were no major rivers in this part of the country at all. Then one day a strange man worked his way up through this region and into the country just to the north, where he found the camp of an old woman who had a huge basket of fish. As the man was very hungry, he asked her if she'd cook him something for dinner. She agreed, but first she got a very serious look on her face, looked the man right in the eye, and told him one thing: "Stay away from my basket of fish."

Well, of course the fellow didn't listen, and while the old woman was cooking he messed with the basket, and eventually stepped on the edge of it and tipped it over. The water started spreading very quickly, and the man ran frantically ahead of it, trying to stop it by piling huge mounds of rocks in its path. The flow reached the first rock pile, broke through it, and created Upper Yellowstone Falls. He ran ahead several more miles, built another dam of rocks, but the water broke through that too, forming the Lower Yellowstone Falls.

At this point the man decided he could do no more to stop that flow, which became the Yellowstone River, so he ran back and tried to stem the current coming from the other side of the basket. He built a huge dam downstream in eastern Idaho, but the water again broke through, this time creating what we know as the Idaho Falls of the Snake River. And on and on he went to the west, building more and more barriers, certain each time this would be the one to stop the water. But the torrent always overwhelmed whatever he threw in its path, first creating American Falls, then Shoshone Falls, and then Twin Falls. Near the Oregon-Idaho border the man built the biggest dam of all between two high hills. But once again the water broke through, and with the power of the boulders in its arms, gouged out Hell's Canyon—the deepest chasm in the country.

If all this sounds like just the kind of trick that a coyote would pull (*ezeppa*, in the Shoshone language), indeed it was. The woman was Mother Earth, and the basket full of fish that coyote tipped over is Yellowstone Lake. Now at first this story may seem sorely out of touch with geography, since the headwaters of the Yellowstone and the Snake rivers rise on opposite sides of the Continental Divide. But not only is Yellowstone Lake thought to be older than the river canyons that lie below it, but many geologists think that several times in the distant past the lake did in fact drain into the Pacific by way of the Snake River.

After sixteen miles of walking we camp in a burned forest on a ledge above Bridger Lake. There is a certain starkness to the land, strangely beautiful, the ghost trees silhouetted against a clear wash of sky, the edges brazed with a bright band of alpenglow. A flock of coots float quietly on the far side of the lake, their soft croaks and cackles drifting easily across the water. Just as we've settled into admiring this tranquil scene, a major rockslide suddenly lets loose somewhere behind us, along the northern edges of Hawk's Rest—hard, deep roars that shatter the quiet; then a brief, shallow trickle, and then utter silence. Even the coots seem to have noticed and stop their chattering. Though such events are hardly unusual in the backcountry, I've always felt like it was a special privilege to be there when they happened, to see or hear a slice of mountain grinding back into the plains from which it came. Once in the sleeping bags we have no trouble drifting off to sleep, though not before hearing the bugle of a young elk across the valley to the west, and then a chorus of coyotes—hoots and yowls and whistles, all floating through the night across the waters of the Yellowstone.

The next morning, a mile or so up Thoroughfare Creek, our path leads us right into a small horse camp. Not wanting to alarm anyone, I holler a greeting, and after a grunt or two from inside a small yellow mountain tent, a man of about forty emerges in his long underwear, smiling, eyes half mast, stubble thick and rough on his tanned face. I notice a plastic sack beside the tent, with ten or fifteen crushed beer cans in it.

"How about a cup of coffee?" he asks us. "God knows I need one."

A few seconds later a woman emerges from the tent, still zipping her pants and tucking in her clothes, blinking hard into the morning light. "I'm Karen," she says to us, sounding far more cheery than she looks.

I apologize several times for getting them up, though they assure us it was the beer the night before that they're having to wrestle with, and not the hour of the day. Over coffee the conversation turns to bears, and the man, whose name is Hale, gets up, goes over to a pack beside a burned tree, and brings back a portable electric fence and a small battery pack, all in a package no more than two feet long and five inches across. "This is what the hunting camp outfitters use," he explains. "Just wrap it around a few trees, and any nosy bear who comes around gets a jolt. Works great. In fact, a guide told me that most bears know what these fences are, and don't bother coming any closer." To me it seems somehow like cheating, though

I can't deny that there have been a few dark nights when all this would have seemed like a fine idea. "Hell," says Hale, "you should carry one in your pack. No worries." Karen quickly agrees, reiterating a story we've heard several times before, that the Thoroughfare country is where the Park Service drops off problem grizzly bears.

Karen is from Jackson Hole, and Hale is a zealous sailing bum from South Africa who's come inland for a change of pace. Most of his year, he explains, is spent caretaking other people's single-hull yachts and catamarans. "On my last job, I basically got paid a lot of money to party in the Hawaiian Islands on a forty-six-foot cat. Of course I had to have it ready for the guy who owned it. But he ran a company in Chicago— did good if he found ten days a year for the water."

Hale then proceeds to tell us of sailing his own vessel up the rivers of Mozambique at a time when the locals "seemed to collect AK-47's," and how, approaching settlements, he'd hide the woman who was with him below decks in order to not "tempt the ruffians into stealing her at gunpoint." And then there are fanciful tales of the Turquoise Coast and Madagascar, of yacht parties off the coast of Turkey, of working for two years as a fisherman for the French Foreign Legion, and in that job visiting islands so remote that "lizards still ran right up to you, and birds would land on your outstretched arms." Of course just how much of all this is true who can say, but there could be worse ways of spending a morning than sitting in this forest in the middle of nowhere, our hands around hot cups of coffee, listening to exotic tales. Much as we'd like to stay, though, we have some tough trail ahead of us. We gulp down the last of the brew, thank our hosts, and trudge off through the burn.

There's no question now that the land has started to drift toward the cold, waiting arms of autumn. Patches of cow parsnip look tired and ragged, and many of the plants have been clipped by grazing elk. The acres and acres of fireweed, which only yesterday was capped with beautiful lavender flower spikes, now show only cottony tufts of seed, and the edges of their leaves are washed in crimson and rust. Plump scarlet fruits, or hips, hang like ornaments from the branches of the wild rose. The bull elk we see seem bold and restless, like young men on city streets, looking for a fight.

Before we left on this particular leg of the trip I made a call to check on our route over the highline of the Absarokas, at a place called Rampart Pass. I had some misgivings because while the trail showed up on an old version of a Bridger-Teton Forest map, on a more recent one it had been removed.

"Well," said a friendly voice on the other end of the phone, "are you on a horse or on foot?"

"We're on foot."

"That's good. 'Cause if you wanna kill a horse, there's no better place to do it than Rampart Pass. It's a real nightmare."

At the time I figured I had someone on the phone who likes to salt and pepper their conversations with a little exaggeration. But much to our amazement, this was clearly not the case. The trail, or perhaps goat path would be a more appropriate term, climbs a staggering 1,800 feet in a single mile. Much of the time we are leaning forward to the point where we can reach out and easily touch the side of the mountain with our fingertips; in fact, I often do just that in order to steady myself while I catch my breath. A third of the way up we find ourselves beside cold, white sprays of water flying past long rock jetties and spilling into tattered mats of moss campion, alpine parsley, gentian, forget-me-nots, and saxifrage. Pikas scurry among boulders stained with patches of rust-colored lichen. Far below is the emerald green meadow where we began, Open Creek now just a thin braid flashing in the sun. And sure enough, in the bottoms of the ravines that lie on either side of the path are the bleached white bones of horses—at least three that we can make out—as well as the remains of one elk, and the skull of a bighorn sheep.

Two-thirds of the way to the top, unable to go more than half a dozen steps without panting like sled dogs in deep snow, we look up to see a female bighorn eyeing us from above. A moment later a youngster, by now probably twelve weeks old, comes scampering up behind her, dancing across the cliff edges as if she were utterly unhinged from the force of gravity.

No doubt there are other sheep just over the ridge, but by the time we grunt our way to the top they will probably be long gone. In a few more weeks the rut will begin, the sound of butting heads ringing like rifle shots across these lonesome mountaintops. (Bighorn are able to engage in such head butting without knocking each other silly thanks in large part to a unique double skull. Contrary to a rumor popular around 1900, however, they cannot escape predators by leaping several hundred feet off of precipices onto their heads!)

Only the victor of the bighorn's autumn duels will copulate with females; in order to keep other rams away, intercourse may take place on a thin lip of rock at the edge of a thousand-foot plunge. When Jane and I finally reach the top of the pass, we catch sight of a dozen more sheep prancing with an easy gait down a thin spine of rock, heading north for the wind-blasted summit of Battlement Mountain.

Rampart Pass is one of those ultimate high country perches—cold and stony, buffeted by winds that stampede across the ice fields and roar up the narrow chutes of rock. Massive, blocky peaks and twisted ridgelines rise in every direction, like an ocean of stone forever frozen into heavy seas. The names of the surrounding peaks are fanciful, yet thoroughly appropriate: Battlement Mountain, Fortress Mountain, Chaos Mountain, Clouds Home Peak. The mix of distance and sheer plunge lines is enough to unseat my sense of balance, to send my mind spinning and weaving in a feeble attempt to calibrate these staggering dimensions. All in all, this seems to be a place more of myth than of any firm reality—Francis Parkman's "mountains silent in primeval sleep."

By the time we descend the 2,200 vertical feet to the head-waters of Rampart Creek, our bodies are frazzled—out of muscle and out of gas. We pull off the packs, set up the stove, and proceed to eat bowl after bowl of carbohydrates—ramen noodles, rice, crackers, fruits. As I eat, it feels as if I'm jump-starting a car that's been sitting idle for months, the system grabbing and lurching at first, and then finally settling into a strong, familiar hum.

We hike for another three miles or so before setting up

camp. By the time we get in it is nearly dark, barely enough light to set up the tent and hang the food. Again we sleep the sleep of the weary. But on this night, thirty minutes or so before dawn breaks, I'm awakened by the one sound outside the tent that I've been afraid of hearing all along. It is most definitely a grunting, snorting sound, not unlike a pig, accompanied now and then by the occasional racket of an old log being torn to pieces in a hunt for insects and grubs. It is, without question, a bear.

Jane opens her eyes, and I put my index finger upright over my lips, and mouth the word "bear." Understandably, she seems a bit startled at first, but then lies back to listen. The next time I look over at her, right after a particularly heart-stopping grunt, she's fallen asleep! This from a woman who last year was so nervous about hiking into grizzly country that her feet would puddle in sweat. I, on the other hand, lie as wide awake as if I'd just finished a No-Doz sandwich and a kettle of cowboy coffee, trying to stifle my fantasies of a giant claw suddenly coming through the flimsy nylon walls of the tent. Because the tent fly is on I can't see anything, and I'm certainly not inclined to poke my head out and draw attention to myself. After ten minutes or so the bear seems to be slowly ambling away. The grunts and snorts get softer and softer, until I'm left listening very hard into total silence, every measure of my attention channeled through my ears, as if by focusing, my hearing might somehow be enhanced to super-human levels. And then a chickadee calls from above, and in the distance a woodpecker does a soft drumroll, and slowly, gratefully, I fall back to sleep.

In fifty miles of walking we have seen only three parties. So it is with some surprise during the next day that we come out of the trailless, rocky chasm of Rampart Creek into Elk Fork wash, and see an old cowboy fly fishing from atop a chalk-colored mare. "How're you folks doing?" he asks, flashing a smile full of yellow teeth, as though he'd been waiting for us all along. "Where've ya been?"

I proceed to give him a quick rundown of our trip. He listens intently, like he's going to have to recite it all back to me, until I get to the part about Rampart Pass being a real workout.

"Hell!" he interrupts, the horse flinching as he leans into the stirrups. "I'm the one who blasted out that route back in the thirties! Drilled holes in the cliffs big enough to shove in a pickaxe handle, blew 'em out with dynamite, and that was the trail. Was outfittin' all over this country then—used to set huntin' camps at the head of Open Creek."

Considering the warnings I was given about taking horses over that pass, I find it incredible that someone would've made a habit of crossing it with pack strings. When I mention the skeletons we saw lying in the ravines the old man just laughs, as if all that was the proof of the kind of bumbling that separates the men from the boys. Later we meet the man's grandson, who tells us that five years ago, at the age of seventy-five, his grandfather took the family on a six-week horse pack trip from Gardiner to Meteetse, Wyoming. "The old fart ran our asses off, too," he says, punctuating the remark with a slow nod.

Before heading off I ask the old man what his secret is. He blinks hard, and then leans down from his horse until his tanned, wrinkled face—eight decades' worth of smiles and weather and squints—is no more than two feet from me. "Good women, good whiskey, and good tobacco." With that he straightens back up, gives me a quick wink, and turns back to the stream to make another cast.

ELEVEN

My journey is winding down, and with it, the end of another mountain summer. The nights are noticeably colder now, and the same storms that bring rain to the valleys leave the high country dusted with snow. Gold- and coral-colored aspen leaves dangle in the wind against cloudless skies, and the deciduous forests run thick with the sweet, sad smell of decay. Major burns from the fires of 1988 make the trek along the North Fork of the Shoshone seem especially blank and barren, yet each day the muddy places along the trail are filled with the tracks of bears and deer and coyotes, and by evening the valleys ring with the sound of bugling elk.

Late one night in a Red Lodge bar, a friend in his forties who has never really backpacked accepts an invitation to join me for three of the final days of trail. This is the same guy, incidentally, who burned his eyebrows off crouching into the fire against the "grizzly from hell" that summer night on Slough Creek. On this trip he sleeps with a pistol close to his pillow, "to shoot myself if a bear comes at me," he jokes. Yet he's hardly reassured when one morning we walk out of camp to find a huge pile of bear scat still steaming on the trail. In fact, it's the rush of that particular discovery that propels him out of the forest and up a fifteen-hundred-foot pass at a re-markable pace. Unfortunately, just as he begins to breathe easy about bears, we meet three sheep hunters coming up the other side, one of whom tells us that at the bottom of the ravine is a line of the biggest grizzly prints he's ever seen in his life. We share a swig of whisky to steel our courage, and down we go. But there are no prints anywhere to be seen, and we conclude that the story was a hoax.

The hundred miles or so of trail I've walked with friends has been a grand part of this adventure. In a culture that has little to offer when it comes to rituals for celebrating friendships, it would be hard to think of a better one than sharing the toil and elation of a journey through the mountains. Feelings of kinship rise easily here, sometimes even with the most casual of acquaintances, who all of a sudden are remarkably willing to talk of things that for some reason are rarely broached within the confines of everyday living. In the backcountry I've heard men who I always thought were emotional stone walls suddenly speaking in hushed tones about some crushing personal loss, and seen them twirling on the tops of mountains like little boys, wired with exhilaration. No wonder people have long used nature walks as vehicles for conversation—from American and Soviet heads of state strolling through the woods of Geneva in talks of peace, to John Muir and Ralph Waldo Emerson, philosophizing in the shade of the Yosemite pines.

The day after seeing the pile of bear scat outside our camp consists of a long, luscious ramble along Sunlight Creek, the rugged parapets of the Absarokas flashing bright in the autumn sun, the stream corridor thick with deer, moose, and beaver. To me this is one of the loveliest, most accessible valleys in the entire Yellowstone ecosystem. But here too the land is checkerboarded with a long line of mineral claims, and may one day soon be lined with tailings piles and settling ponds.

While land management agencies are allowing more and more heavy extractive uses of this ecosystem, the science needed to gain better understanding of the cumulative effects of the projects is still in its infancy. In fact the only cumulative-effects model being used with any regularity at all is for a single species, the grizzly, and even in that case formulae for determining things like human-related mortality and displacement aren't fully developed. In the interim we deal out leases and hope for the best, ignoring the cautions of experienced biologists because they lack the hard numbers to prove their claims.

It is now the final day of walking. Four of us are on an easy amble across the ten-thousand-foot Line Creek Plateau, beneath a dazzling wash of autumn sky. This is the largest run of alpine tundra in the continental United States, and today the dried, hazel-colored grasses and forbs spread like a prairie dream across the rooftop of the world. Over my left shoulder are the calm but massive swells of the Hell Roaring Plateau, with Mount Rearguard and Beartooth Mountain rising from behind like tidal waves of gray stone. Over my right shoulder the land runs to the edge of the plateau and then plunges into a puzzle of dry mesas and twisted ravines, the Clarks Fork River running through northern Wyoming like a thin line of silver throwing back the sun.

Incredibly, here too, just a stone's throw from the road that Charles Kuralt once called the most beautiful highway in America, there looms the distinct possibility of oil derricks being planted on the tundra sometime in the not too distant future. Even though this district of the Custer National Forest is one of the most heavily used recreation areas in the country, though the ecosystem is so fragile that a few miles away the Forest Service has refused to allow even mountain bikes on it, there continues to be strong pressure for oil and gas development by both industry and a prodevelopment executive branch of government. In 1991, pressure was exerted by the Bush administration to study every nonwilderness acre on both the Custer and the Shoshone for possible oil and gas development.

It's been fifteen years since I first started writing about nature and the environment, and by now I consider myself somewhat hard to unnerve. Yet today I stand on this plateau, which, for sheer, glorious breadth is truly as fine a place as

any I've ever known, utterly confounded that we would seriously consider losing it to development. If we cannot save
even this, despite a clear mandate to do so expressed through
hundreds of letters and comments during and after input
meetings with the Forest Service, despite petitions with thousands of signatures from residents of the region and visitors
from around the world, then truly there is little hope left for
the American landscape. Indeed, the entire Yellowstone ecosystem makes up but a scant 0.5 percent of the continental
United States, yet today much of it seems destined to fold
under the weight of overindustrializaton. This is not progress.
This is selling the soul of the American West for a bag of beans.

So-called "wise use" groups would have us believe that
opening places like Line Creek Plateau to development is nothing less than the patriotic thing to do. (During one public
input meeting on the Greater Yellowstone Vision Document,
a woman wearing the yellow armband of the prodevelopment
forces signed up to speak, and then recited the pledge of al-
legiance.) But in the late 1700s, when this country was young
and hopeful and desperate to anchor itself to some source of
national pride, it was largely our wilderness that buoyed us
up, that became one of the strongest calls to American patri-
otism. We had, after all, little to offer when it came to art and
architecture, especially compared to the rich treasures of Europe. What we did have were wild places of staggering beauty
and proportion. And to many of the greatest thinkers of the
day, it was those wild places that represented the foundation
from which an entire culture would eventually find the in-
spiration to fashion its identity.

Carl Jung once wrote that in the United States the land
seemed to have a strange, dramatic impact on a person's psyche—something that in the end he could only attribute to
"the mystery of the American earth." The great Revolutionary
War general Lafayette was so enamored of American soil that
he had a box of it shipped back to France to be buried in. It
was the enormous possibilities that hovered just beyond the
edges of the frontier, and not the settlements themselves, that
brought such an intoxicating level of intrigue to the minds

and hearts of the country, that launched countless books and paintings, and etchings from the house of Currier and Ives.

The tendency of the masses to swashbuckle through the wilderness was not so much indicative of a need to eradicate it, as it was based on the assumption that there would always be enough of it to go around. In 1910, when conservationists were pushing for creation of Glacier National Park, some politicians thought the idea preposterous. "It seems to be protected by nature without our setting it aside," explained one senator. "It is practically inaccessible." Seventy years later, in a comprehensive survey of the national park system, Glacier was listed as the most beleaguered of all American parks, with fifty-six identified threats to its integrity. And now Yellowstone is close behind. If history has any bearing on the future at all, it suggests that all lands not properly managed or protected now will be lost or severely degraded in the decades to come.

How much longer can we ignore the ticking clock? How good will we become at squelching the notion that the passion and spirit of the land that nursed us for so much of our history was something of real value? For politicians who believe that federal lands ought to be little more than profit grounds for extractive industry, it's as if it's still 1880, and we're all sixteen years old. They continue to stump for resource development, when in this region alone recreation jobs are outpacing those of mining and logging by four to one. They claim that wilderness is bad for the economy because it locks up resources, when a recent study of nine counties in western Montana that have large wilderness areas found that they were growing at a rate more than three times the state average. Collectively, they seem to be proving Tocqueville right. "I know of no country," he wrote of America in 1835, "where the love of money has taken stronger hold on the affections of men, and where a profounder contempt is expressed for the theory of the permanent equality of property."

A few years ago, *Omni* magazine published the results of a challenge the magazine made to advertising agencies across the country to develop ads that would help sell the concept of space exploration. Among the winners, submitted by one of the top advertising agencies in the country, was a piece depicting the evolutionary stages of man. On the far left was a drawing of an ape on all fours, followed left to right by eight more figures, each one looking more and more like a modern *homo sapiens*. The last drawing was of a nearly hairless, thoroughly up-to-date fellow, not gazing straight ahead, as the other figures had been doing, but at the sky. At the top of the image, in bold white letters, it read: "WHAT MAKES US THE MOST INTELLIGENT SPECIES ON EARTH IS KNOWING THAT WE MUST LEAVE IT TO SURVIVE."

The message seems clear. We don't evolve by learning from our mistakes; we evolve by figuring out ways to outrun them. Herman Melville once said that there is something very wrong with a man's religion when it makes the earth an uncomfortable place for him to be. In a secular culture like ours, the same might be said of his technology.

TWELVE

I think the greatest insight I ever had into the power of nature came several years ago, when my mother lay bedridden, dying of cancer. Having for a month been too weak to even hold her head up, one day she announced that she wanted to go outside. So I carefully gathered her up in my arms and carried her through the front door and out into the yard. Around we went for what must have been twenty minutes—first so she could smell the flowers on her lilac bushes, then so she could look through the woods above the bird feeder for the flash of a certain cardinal's wings, and finally, so she could run the supple young leaves of the maples and dogwoods through her fingers.

I still wonder at the solace she managed to gather from that final dance through her special patch of sprouting ground. Having over the months watched disease whittle her soft, round body into something sharp and breakable, having seen the light in her eyes fade behind a wall of morphine, I was finding it hard to buy the claims of the Crow and the Sioux, who believe that a person is never more powerful than when she is about to die. But on that day she *was* powerful. By no small miracle she was somehow able to harness the mystery floating through that quarter-acre yard and use it to light the dark place that was closing in around her. That afternoon the pain that she'd worn for so long began draining from her face, replaced by a look of serenity that I'd never seen in her, even when she was young and healthy. The next morning she told us to stop all of her painkillers, this after being on massive doses of Percocet and morphine for several months. A few days later, in the wee, still hours of the night, she drifted away.

The flash of that cardinal, those soft green leaves of the maple and the dogwood, are small, precious hints of the wild tapestry that once circled the earth, the patterns and paradigms that first breathed meaning into human existence. For many people those hints are what help transcend the tumult of daily living, they are that slim measure of miracle that brings wholeness to a severed world. Looking back, I realize that I too was hunting for such inklings, such assurances, from the nooks and crannies of the Yellowstone. And what is perhaps most remarkable of all is that I never once failed to find them.

Winter has returned again to the Yellowstone Rockies. Goats are roaming the icy ledges of the Beartooth Plateau, while elk in shaggy hides huddle on the winter range. The Yellowstone River slips quietly eastward across the plains under thick sheets of ice. Cold north winds push hard against the trees, hissing through the gnarled fingers of the aspen and the cottonwood.

In the land of long ago this would have been the time to gather in the winter lodges and tell stories—tales of coyotes, of the stars, of the rivers and the birds. More than just idle storytelling, though, winter lore was a way of rekindling the fires of the old myths, of both affirming and teaching to the next generation the coordinates of the world that could be used to steer a life by. When spring arrived most of the storytelling came to an end, not to resume again until the following winter. Perhaps in these other months the people were too busy hunting and gathering food or making clothes and tools to share stories. On the other hand, maybe when the blooms of the pasqueflower first lay on the prairie in spring, through the time when the last elk bugle drifted through the forest, the tales of the earth were somehow enough.

What kind of stories will we have to tell of this place in the years to come? Will they rise out of an earth still alive with beauty and danger, or will they merely be reminiscences of things long since lost to the world? For all the gold and platinum and lumber we may take from the Yellowstone Rockies in the years to come, we can never rebuild the strange and urgent mystery of these lands. Of this place that helps us heal. Of this place that lets us dance.